So May It Be

כן יהי רצון

Reflections on what really matters

Rabbi Randy Kafka

So May It Be:
Reflections on what really matters

Copyright © 2015 by Randy R. Kafka

In gratitude to all my teachers,
especially Art Green

Contents

Introduction

Each year, in preparation for the high holidays, I go through a process of discerning which issues feel most *alive* to me. What is happening in the world? In the community? What would it take courage for me to talk about?

Sometimes I end up with one theme for all four of the holiday sermons; sometimes not. My ultimate goal is for each sermon to be a *gift* to those who in turn give me the gift of their attention and trust.

This book contains my high holiday sermons from Yom Kippur 2010 through Yom Kippur 2014. They were written to be spoken, which is different than an essay that is written to be read silently; so if you know me, try to hear my voice as you read. If you don't know me, try reading them aloud to yourself!

And may they be a gift for you as well.

כן יהי רצון / *So may it be.*

Guaranteed Wake-Up Call

Kol Nidrei 2010

You're not supposed to take things from hotel rooms. Everybody knows that, right?

Well... this past June we were in New Jersey to celebrate my mother's 80th birthday, and I saw something in the hotel room that I just had to have.

Not to worry, though... I went downstairs to the front desk to ask permission first, and they said it was okay.

I've been saving it to share with you tonight, because it is the perfect symbol of what this holy day of Yom Kippur is all about: "Guaranteed Wake-Up Call."

That's it. That's the whole message of Yom Kippur. This is your guaranteed wake-up call.

Life is full of wake-up calls. Let me name just a few from my own experiences this past year – hearing from a friend that his seemingly-perfect life is unraveling from alcoholism and other addictions in the family... my husband Alan's emergency heart surgery a year-ago Rosh Hashanah... the magnitude 8.8 earthquake which rocked Chile weeks after I happened to be in Santiago for a friend's wedding.

On another level, there are events which are wake-up calls even if we imagine that we are not directly affected: for example, the gulf oil spill disaster... or the suicide of a teenager in Easton this summer.

We all hear wake-up calls, don't we? Even if they haven't hit us directly – yet – they are whispering in our ears as they brush past us.

Take a moment now and think of a wake-up call you have experienced or heard about this past year.

Yom Kippur is one of those wake-up calls, too. The question is: Wake up to what?

Wake up to death is the most obvious first answer. Did you know that Yom Kippur was designed by the ancient rabbis to be an annual rehearsal of our death? There are many intentional parallels between Yom Kippur and death. It is customary to wear white on Yom Kippur – because at our death we will be buried in plain white shrouds. We recite the confessional prayer on Yom Kippur, the vidui – which is also recited before death. And we fast and abstain from various other physical pleasures on Yom Kippur, some say to mimic the angels in heaven who have no need for material sustenance – again, an allusion to our death.

I know that some of you have experienced the death of a loved one recently, or are facing life-and-death issues in your family right now. So perhaps for you there is no need for the wake-up call of Yom Kippur. You've received yours already.

Stark as it may sound, our ancient sages understood that the primary work to be done in this holiday season is dying – metaphorically, by letting go of our illusions of being in control; and literally, by waking up to

10

death's inevitability and unpredictability.

Thus the primary action of the high holidays is not this [fist on heart]. The primary action of the high holidays is this – [opening the fist]

Again, the question: Wake up to what? Here is another answer: *Wake up to life.*

There is another wake-up call system built into Jewish tradition which you may be less familiar with. Understanding Judaism as a system of spiritual practices, we begin to see that *everything* we do has the potential to wake us up to life.

What does it mean that Judaism is a system of spiritual practices? Judaism is fundamentally not about what we believe, but about what we DO, and about how that doing transforms us.

A simple example of a Jewish spiritual practice: saying a bracha, a blessing, before we eat something. Never mind getting the Hebrew words right – you can always learn that later – the simple practice of STOPPING and NOTICING before we dive into our food is the essence of the practice. (Forgive me for talking about food on Yom Kippur, but it's still early enough in the fast not to be frustrating!)

Here's how it works: Just before you are about to eat or drink something, STOP and take a really careful look at – and whiff of – what you are about to eat or drink. Examine the colors, the textures, the symmetry or asymmetry. The fractal patterns in one tiny piece of broccoli… the bubbles at the top of a glass of milk and how the light reflects off them... whatever it is, just notice the astonishing beauty of it.

Or you might ponder for a moment the infinite web of events and actions involving millions of people around the planet that led to this particular food appearing in front of you at this particular moment.

You might also contemplate the wonders of ingestion and digestion, the miraculous processes by which this food will be converted into fuel for your body.

The more you are aware, the more everyday events like this appear to be wondrous miracles. This is the practice of saying a bracha, of expressing gratitude for the miracles which we daily take for granted. This is the practice of waking up to life, and it can happen at any moment.

Do I remember to do this *every* time I eat? No. But that's why we call it "practice"!

All of these things I'm saying, I am of course saying to myself as well. Which is why I believe that we need spiritual community. We need to support one another in our efforts to wake up. We need to be spirit buddies for one another. How will we take on this challenge in the coming year, you and I?

There are wake-up calls all around us, calls to wake up to the reality of death AND to the reality of life.

This is true for us as individuals, and this is true for our two temples that are now one.

A new year and a new temple. Both are about loss,

and possibility. Both are about endings and beginnings. Both are about regrets and dreams. Both are about death – and rebirth.

There is some truth in the perception that our two little temples have died. We should not ignore the reality that some people feel that way, and there is no shame in that. There is a sense of loss for some people – which I understand as the loss of the hope that what once was, many years ago, could somehow be restored.

And yet... Nothing lives forever. Not people, not temples. Nothing new can be born without something dying. There is no spring and summer without fall and winter.

I once attended a talk by one of Alan's earth science colleagues, who said something so striking that I wrote it down and saved it. In speaking about the extinctions that occurred on the planet some 580 million years ago, he said that the extinctions were a great thing because they cleared the way for an explosion of new life.

Death. Life. Two sides of one reality. We might say that the challenge then is to wake up to both life *and* death, which may be another way of saying wake up to God.

The great medieval rabbinic philosopher and physician Maimonides wrote: "Awake, you sleepers, from your slumber! ... And remember your creator, you who forget the truth amidst the pursuit of emptiness, wasting all your days in emptiness that neither profits nor saves."

The shofar is our alarm clock. Yom Kippur is our wake -up call. There are wake-up calls sounding all around us, in every moment. We can hear the call, and respond... or we can hit SNOOZE. Which will it be?

Sorry Rabbi, I Don't Believe in God

Yom Kippur 2010

I had a wonderful long talk about God recently with a seven-year-old friend of mine, who gave me permission to mention our conversation today. I had asked her to meet with me over the summer because I needed her help in thinking through how to talk about God.

My little friend told me that sometimes before she falls asleep she wrestles with the question of whether or not God exists. She then articulated for me the logic she was using: Either such-and-such is true, in which case God exists; or such-and-such is true, in which case God does *not* exist. It sounded like it was only a matter of time before she would come to a logical conclusion.

As I listened, and as I heard the either/or nature of the logic, I tentatively offered her what I had been thinking about, as another way of framing the question of God's existence. Then together we played around with ways to say it that would be understandable and useful. I hoped that this alternate way of framing the question would perhaps liberate her from the forced choice she was headed towards.

What I would like to offer to all of you today, on this holiest of holy days, is a similar possibility of liberation.

Liberation from what? Liberation from a deep misunderstanding about God. Liberation from a deep misunderstanding about *belief* in God, that has been a stumbling block for the Jewish people for a couple of hundred years.

What I have to say today may sound radical to some of you, and it is, in the sense that the word radical means "of or having roots." This message of liberation is rooted in Jewish tradition going back thousands of years.

I know that many of you are in need of liberation, because I have heard it many times: "Sorry, Rabbi. I don't believe in God." Or "Sorry, Rabbi. My teenager just announced that she doesn't believe in God, and frankly I can't really argue with her."

You instinctively say "Sorry, Rabbi" because deep down you believe that to be a good Jew, you *ought* to believe in God. Right? And you believe that of all people, of course the Rabbi does believe in God. Right?

So here is my first radical statement of liberation to those of you who don't believe in God: *The God that you don't believe in, I don't believe in either.* So you have nothing to apologize for!

Let me summarize the God that many of you don't believe in. My apologies in advance to those of you who do believe in this God that I am about to describe. And please keep listening, because I want you to hear that there is an alternative – and that in the end, being Jewish is not about what you believe anyway! *Being Jewish is not about what you believe.*

The God that many of you don't believe in is the biblical, personal God. This is the God who *does* things, who listens and responds, who is sort of like a very large, very powerful invisible *person,* only somehow more so. It is the God who speaks from a burning bush, the God who splits the sea so the Israelites can walk through on dry ground, the God who answers (or perversely doesn't answer) personal prayers... the God who should have saved us from the Holocaust but didn't. It is the God that doesn't make logical sense to a thoughtful older child, and is therefore so often rejected as "not existing" by the time of bat or bar mitzvah. It is the God that leads thoughtful people like you to conclude that religion is naïve, and that only science can be trusted as a map of reality.

But what if I told you that there is an alternative Jewish vision of God? – a vision of God that is compatible with science, critical thinking and rationality, and which yet encompassing our experience of mystery, awe and wonder?

I won't go into the various historical factors and occurrences that led to the situation we are in, but suffice it to say that a major thread of Jewish tradition was snipped out of the tapestry and almost lost a couple of hundred years ago. Since then, we have been "sold a bill of goods" about God that is missing this precious thread.

So what *is* God, if not the biblical personal God we learned of as a child?

First of all, "God" isn't a Jewish word. The primary Jewish word for God is yud-hey-vav-hey, a series of four Hebrew consonants without vowels, which sounds like a breath when you try to say it out loud.

YHVH. We say "Adonai" (my Lord) when we come to this word in the text because it is traditionally unpronounceable. This four-letter name is an impossible grammatical form of the verb "to be." The best possible translation is perhaps "Is-Was-Will Be" all at once.

In the words of my teacher Rabbi Arthur Green, YHVH is "the wholeness of being, the energy that makes for existence, the engine that drives the evolutionary process." It is the "inner force of existence itself," "the animating spirit of the whole great evolutionary journey."*

In other words – recognizing that words can only take us so far – God is Reality with a capital R, unfathomable, mysterious. God is all there is. God is not a being, God is Being with a capital B.

This is an ancient perspective. For example, we sing in the Aleinu prayer: "Ka-katuv b'torato, v'yadat ha-yom v'hashevota el l'vavecha – Ki Adonai hu ha-elohim ba-shamayim mi-ma'al. V'al ha-a'retz mi-tachat – ain ohd." Which means: "As it is written in the Torah: know this day, and place it on your heart, that YHVH is God in heaven and beyond, on the earth and below – there is nothing else." Ain ohd – *there is nothing else.* There it is – hiding in plain sight in our prayerbooks behind a chirpy little tune. And you'll see it elsewhere, once you start looking.

Some of you may have come to this sense of Oneness through a spiritual experience, or through exploration in Buddhist meditation or yoga or some other non-Western path. My message of liberation to *you* today is that you don't need to say "Sorry Rabbi, I'm not religious – I'm spiritual." Because this belief in and experience of Oneness is not only found in other cultures, but is deeply rooted in Judaism as well. We have it in our own religious "tool kit," it's just that it has been buried out of sight for the past few centuries.

I believe that it is also possible to come to this perspective through reason, as well as through study and contemplation.

Now, what about all these WORDS in the prayerbook? Aren't we supposed to believe them?? Avinu Malkeinu, we sing on the high holidays, which means: Our Father, Our King. Who – or what – do we imagine we are praying to?

There is an expression used by our ancient sages that "the Torah is written in the language of humans" – meaning that it uses ordinary language to express the un-express-able, to point us towards deeper truths.

The Torah was never meant to be read literally. Never. Literalism is a fairly new phenomenon historically, and decidedly un-Jewish. The words of the Torah and our liturgy are all attempts by people who have experienced the reality of God in their lives to point us in that direction using metaphor and poetry. To take their words literally is a big mistake. We believe that our scriptures speak the truth, but not that they are *literally* true. They are gateways to truth.

At the same time, our tradition has always acknowl- edged the deeply felt need we have to be in *relation-*

ship with something greater than ourselves. Out of this need, we have *personified* God, projecting human attributes so that we can feel ourselves to be in relationship with that which animates us. We say baruch atah Adonai – blessed are *you* YHVH – not because God is a person, but because *we* are relational beings.

As with any attempt to talk about God, at some point words become stumbling blocks – so I will stop at this point and shift to my final question: What is the practical significance of all of this? Let me suggest three possibilities:

First, I am on a campaign to advocate that "Do you believe in God?" is not a Jewish question!

There's a joke about this. When asked "do you believe in God?", the appropriate response is: Do I believe in God? It depends what you mean by "God," it depends what you mean by "believe," and it depends what you mean by "I." I find this to be very funny, and at the same time very deep and true.

In the end it doesn't matter what you believe that God is or isn't. *Judaism isn't about believing, it's about doing!* Jewish spiritual practices – including the recitation of prayers using God language – are all designed to *take* us somewhere, to alter our consciousness you might say. So if you are not actively "doing Jewish," you are missing the point.

Second, if everything in existence is a manifestation of that dynamic force which we refer to as God, then it follows that everything in existence is deserving of respect and care. To say that all people are "made in the image of God" is not a statement about physical resemblance – as if God had arms and legs – but is rather pointing towards the truth that we too are manifestations of that dynamic force which we refer to as God – and from this worldview springs the ethical imperative to deal justly and mercifully with all people equally.

And a third practical implication – Young children may have more natural access than we do to the experience of the Oneness of all things. They *live* awe and wonder and mystery on a daily basis. We in fact have much to learn from them.

How can we support our children – and ourselves – in rejecting a narrow *idea* of God without mistakenly believing that we are really rejecting God and Judaism? How can we share with our children – as we explore it ourselves – the ways in which our Jewish spiritual tool kit can deepen our awareness of Reality with a capital R?

My conversation about God with my little friend this summer went on for about 20 or 30 minutes, until she got shpilkes [antsy] and wanted to show me her cartwheels and backbends and swimming dives off the park bench where we were sitting. Such conversations are so precious. I hope to have more of them, with all of you. Being alive is such a grand mystery. Let's explore it together, while we can.

* *Radical Judaism: Rethinking God and Tradition*, Arthur Green, Yale University Press 2010. Art's teachings were the inspiration for this sermon, and many others.

Moving Forward into the Unknown

Erev Rosh Hashanah 2011

Here is a story that we Jews have been telling for thousands of years:

Once there was a man named Avram (later Avraham/ Abraham), who lived in the region of ancient Mesopotamia. Avram became convinced that there was only one all-powerful God, maker of heaven and earth, and that this one invisible and un-nameable God was calling him to leave his home, move to a promised land he did not yet know, and share his faith with the people he would encounter along the way.

You're familiar with that story, right?

Here is another story, that you've probably never heard:

Moses Menachem Zieve came to the United States in the early 1880s from Lithuania. He left behind, to follow him six years later, his wife and four children. After working in New York, Chicago, and Los Angeles, he settled in Minneapolis with his family and, for a livelihood, turned to peddling.

Zieve's territory was the area out of Northfield, Minnesota, forty miles south of Minneapolis. When he set out on his trips he carried with him on his wagon, in addition to his goods for sale, his own utensils for preparing meals in accordance with the requirements of kashrut.

Many week-ends he could not return to Minneapolis

and spent Shabbat at the home of a friendly Christian farmer. He would arrive at the farmer's house on Friday in time to slaughter a chicken, do his Shabbat cooking, and make his personal preparations for Shabbat. In the farmer's home, he observed Shabbat in the traditional manner until the farmer's son reported three stars in the sky on Saturday night.

The German immigrants who settled that area around Northfield worshipped together in a community church. For lack of funds, they had no regular preacher. On Sunday mornings, then, in this community church, Moses Menachem Zieve occupied the pulpit and preached to this German-speaking congregation. His language? A carefully selected non-Hebraic Yiddish. His subjects? The Torah portion of the week. And in serving this Christian community, Zieve won their gratitude – and an affectionate but reverent title. They called him "Holy Moses."*

Lech lecha. The imperative "GO!" that propelled our mythic ancestor Abraham out of his father's home, out of the land of his birth, to a land and a life that he did not yet know.

Lech lecha. The inner and outer circumstances that propelled millions of Jews to leave their homelands and journey to the promised land of America, in search of a better life.

These two stories have much in common, as we – both children and adults – are in the midst of exploring in

Tikvah Learning this semester.

This holiday period between Rosh Hashanah and Yom Kippur is known collectively as the Days of Awe. It is an opportunity for each of us to open up and hear our own *Lech lecha* – the call to move forward into the unknown. The call to move forward despite the lack of certainty about where we are going:

To move forward in search of a new job.

To move forward from an empty or emptying nest.

To move forward out of the nest and into high school, or college, or graduate school.

To move forward within a long-term relationship.

To move forward after a significant relationship has ended.

To move forward after the loss of a loved one.

How do we find the courage and the strength to move forward into the unknown? How do we live with uncertainty? These are some of the questions that we will be exploring during these days of awe.

Lech lecha – for some of us, this imperative GO! may be heard on a physical or a practical level. It's time to move to a new home. It's time to make that doctor's appointment. It's time to go back to school.

And for some of us, this imperative GO! may be heard more on an internal or spiritual level:

Perhaps our habitual ways of relating to family members aren't working for us anymore, because our family members have changed and we haven't.

Perhaps our habitual political beliefs have boxed us into a narrow corner where we are no longer open to new and potentially contradictory information.

Perhaps our habitual certainty that *our* perspective is the *right* one has distanced us from the people around us.

I began with the biblical story of Abraham hearing the Lech lecha call to journey to a new homeland. There is only one other occurrence of the expression Lech lecha in the Torah, and it occurs in the story that is traditionally read in some synagogues on Rosh Hashanah – the story of Abraham hearing a call to bring his son Isaac to the top of a mountain for a sacrifice. Lech lecha, Abraham hears God calling. Take your son, and go. The language of this ancient myth is filled with ambiguity and mystery. As you may recall, just at the moment when it appears that Abraham is about to kill his son Isaac, he stops (or is it that an angel stops him?) and offers up a ram instead. There is a little-known, ancient rabbinic tradition that suggests that Isaac's soul actually departed in that terrifying moment – that he really did die – and was then resurrected. Ambiguity and mystery are at the heart of our foundational myths.

The Torah says that Abraham was tested in that encounter – It is an open question to this day whether Abraham passed the test, or failed the test. It all depends on what we imagine the test to be.

Lech lecha. It is a call from life, to each of us. A call to move forward into the unknown. A call to move forward despite the lack of certainty about where we are going. Perhaps we too are being tested. What is the test? We can never be sure.

I hope you too will take this opportunity to ponder some of the questions raised by this holiday theme of living with uncertainty. How does uncertainty play out in your own life?

Beginning our exploration of uncertainty, I want to suggest that you spend some time over the next few days looking back over the past year, since last Rosh Hashanah. This is a great opportunity for a conversation with family members and/or friends. What plans did you make this past year that didn't turn out the way you had hoped or intended? What uncertainties have you had anxiety over? Have you experienced any unexpected, life-altering occurrences?

Everything about life is uncertain, except the certainty of change.

Lech lecha. It is a call from life, to each of us. A call to move forward into the unknown.

May we all be blessed this year to open our hearts to this call. May we find the courage and the strength to move forward into the unknown. To face life's uncertainties with grace and wisdom.

כן יהי רצון / *So may it be.*

---

* From *The Jew in the American World: A Source Book*, ed. Jacob Rader Marcus, Wayne State University Press 1996

We Just Don't Know

Rosh Hashanah 2011

Recently, Alan and I had reason to be in Logan Airport. As is our custom, we were there early, and thus had plenty of time to sit in the waiting area at our gate. Our attention was caught by a young woman – a *very* young woman – sitting alone with no carry-on except for one oversized garment bag with the name of a bridal shop on it. She also was there very early, but she was crying. Weeping, I should say. When we finally boarded the plane, the captain came on the PA system to tell us that there was a special passenger with us today – a "little girl" who had missed her flight earlier in the day and was therefore missing the rehearsal dinner for her own wedding. He asked us to give her a round of applause to show our support.

We can witness a scene like this, and nod our heads wisely. We think we see the bigger picture, and we can be patronizingly sympathetic. Poor thing, she thinks this is a huge catastrophe, but she is young still. This is really nothing to cry about. After all, she isn't missing her *wedding*. And *really*, it's not like anyone *died*.

I bring this story as colorful illustration, but we could all cite countless examples from our own lives, examples both trivial and profound. We are *every day* confronted with the limits of our ability to know what is happening, and to know what will be happening. To us, and to the people we care about. And sometimes we too are brought to tears.

And yet, it seems to be human nature to *plan*, to imagine that we know what is happening and what will be happening… to *project* our hopes and desires into the future. Planning day after day, year after year.

And it seems also to be human nature that we *suffer* when things do not turn out the way we had planned or hoped. Suffering day after day, year after year.

There are the daily uncertainties, the mundane not-knowings that often occupy our thoughts and generate our anxieties:

How will my child handle being in college for the first time? (And how will *I* handle it?)

How well am I going to do on the midterm, or at the basketball game, or on the SATs?

Is my boss going to approve of my latest project?

Will my new teachers like me?

Will this traffic make me miss my appointment?

Is my loved one's illness going to get better or worse?

These are the daily uncertainties. And then there are the Black Swans. What is a Black Swan? A Black Swan is an occurrence which is unexpected, unpredictable, and carries an extreme impact.

Here is a more detailed definition from the book *The Black Swan*, by Nassim Taleb: "First, it is an *outlier*, as it lies outside the realm of regular expectations, because nothing in the past can convincingly point to its possibility. Second, it carries an extreme impact. Third, in spite of its outlier status, human nature makes us concoct explanations for its occurrence *after* the fact, [in a vain effort to make] it explainable and predictable [in retrospect]."

Real examples of Black Swans in our lives:

The economy tanks and you lose your job.

You meet the love of your life, and they live in another state.

Your spouse leaves you, or dies before they are old.

You go to adopt a child and end up with two, or three.

You invent something that can save lives.

A Black Swan is an event that alters our life's trajectory. That changes our destiny. That catapults us into another reality. And they are happening every day.

Unexpected. Unpredictable. Extreme impact.

I've mentioned examples of personal Black Swans. There are also global Black Swans: Could anyone have predicted the timing of the development of the internet? A Black Swan. Could anyone have predicted the "Arab Spring" uprisings this year? Or the "Israeli Summer" social justice protests? All Black Swans.

The history of the Jewish people is filled with Black Swans. Let me name one of the earliest known examples:

About 3300 years ago, a rag-tag little tribe of Semites

showed up in the tiny middle-east region of Canaan telling anyone who would listen that their invisible God with an unpronounceable name had made it possible for them to escape from slavery in Egypt. Their conviction was so compelling that thousands of polytheistic Canaanites joined them in worshipping this one invisible God... and Judaism evolved out of this merging of cultures.

It was a Black Swan. It was an unexpected event that could not have been predicted, and it had a huge impact on the course of human history. And of course the ancient Israelites explained it by saying that God had made it all happen.

This biblical habit of explaining all events as having been the doings of God can be off-putting to the modern ear. So let me put it another way: Saying "God did it" was our ancestors' way of expressing what they had learned from experience: *We don't know. We cannot know.* They dealt with the uncertainty of not-knowing by *projecting* knowing onto a distant God: We cannot know everything, but there must be someone who does. It must be that God knows everything.

I want to suggest that we in the 21st century can take back this projection – recognize it, own it – and still keep the wisdom behind it. God isn't Up There or Out There somewhere. Whenever you are tempted to pointed upward, try pointing inward instead. There is within us the one who knows what is real and who sees reality clearly. There is within us the one who knows the limits of our knowing.

A famous Yiddish proverb: *Mensch tracht, Gott lacht* – A person plans, God laughs.

What does that mean, really? This is not a statement about God. It is not suggesting that there is a Person Up There who is laughing at us. Such an image of God would be both naïve and offensive. Rather, this is an observation about the human experience. For some of us, it might be better translated as: A person plans, and Reality laughs. There is within us the one who knows what is real and who sees reality clearly... and who chuckles lovingly when we once again are tripped up by our own anxieties.

How does all of this play out in the drama of the High Holidays?

God is King. *Ha-melech ha-yoshev al kiseh ram v'nisah.* The King who sits on the high and exalted throne. Our holiday prayerbook is filled with this God-is-King language... and it is perhaps the biggest turn-off to modern Jews: What are we, medieval serfs? Isn't Judaism more enlightened than that? Or at least more democratic? We are turned off by the suggestion that we are servants, or that there is someone up in the clouds who has power over us.

If we assume that our ancestors meant this image literally, then we have to reject it. And where does that leave us? Holding a book filled with words that we don't believe, alternately bored and angered by those words, yet still vaguely hoping for some sort of "spiritual" feeling.

There must be a better way.

Some of my colleagues have attempted to give this God-is-King language a gentler spin. They say: Oh, the writers of these prayers had in mind a benevolent, loving sort of monarch, concerned for the well-being of "His" subjects. So it's about love, not fear.

I don't know about you, but for me that doesn't help. Benevolent and loving sounds nice, but it is still assuming that there is a Someone Up There who is ultimately in charge.

But listen: If we hear it as metaphor – which I believe was the authors' original intention – then we needn't reject it. We can understand it as another expression of our ancestors' experience of uncertainty and not-knowing. We can hear them reasoning: Maybe we cannot know and are therefore not in control, but there must be someone who does know, and who is in control. It must be that God is in control. God the King is in control.

And once again, I believe that once we see the projection, we can reclaim it. There is *within* us that "sovereign" who knows what is real and who sees reality clearly. There is within us the one who knows the limits of our knowing.

I want to take this one step further. It seems to me that any expression of certainty is at its root an expression of arrogance. It is, in a sense, "playing God." Expressing certainty is a denial of the reality of the human condition. I believe that this is one of the diseases of our time: The airwaves are filled to overflowing with "talking heads" and "empty suits" who claim – 24/7 – to know what is happening and what will be happening. But they don't know, and they can't know. *Mentsch tracht, Gott lacht.* Only this time it's no laughing matter – we all suffer from the consequences of such arrogance.

One final note about uncertainty. As many of you know, last week the president of the Palestinian Authority applied to the United Nations to grant Palestine status as a member nation. Whether or not you have already formed an opinion about how this will affect Israel and the Jewish people, consider this: WE CANNOT KNOW what the consequences of this process will be. We cannot know whether this is fortune or misfortune. No matter how much the talking heads rant and threaten and attempt to frighten us, we cannot know what the consequences of this process will be. No one knows.

And I would like to humbly suggest that it is only out of that place of not-knowing that new possibilities for peaceful coexistence can emerge, both in the Middle East and here at home. In the words of the famous Israeli poet Yehuda Amichai:

From the place where we are right
Flowers will never grow
In the spring.

The place where we are right

Is hard and trampled
Like a courtyard.

But doubts and loves
Dig up the world
Like a mole, like a plow.
And a whisper will be heard in the place
Where the ruined
House once stood.

As we enter this new year 5772, may our *doubts* and our *loves* dig up the world and create the space for new possibilities – for ourselves, for the Jewish people, and for all people everywhere.

כן יהי רצון / *So may it be.*

Do We Have Control
Or Don't We?

Kol Nidrei 2011

The story is told that when Solomon became king of Israel he had a ring made, upon which he had engraved the words *gam zeh ya'avor* – This too shall pass.

Gam zeh ya'avor. This too shall pass. An expression of the truth of life that is both saddening and liberating. Or, in the words of Abraham Lincoln when he told a version of this same story: "This too shall pass. How much it expresses! How chastening in the hour of pride! How consoling in the depths of affliction!"

Gam zeh ya'avor. This too shall pass.

Everything about life is uncertain, except the certainty of change. Everything that we "have" will eventually and inevitably pass away. Slip through our fingers. And tightening our grip doesn't make any difference; it only gives us rope burn.

Everything about life is uncertain, except the certainty of change. Why is it so very difficult for us to grasp that reality? We suffer so much because we don't grasp that reality. Actually, "grasping" may be the wrong image. "Letting go into" that reality might be more like it. Why is it so very difficult for us to let go into the reality of uncertainty and change?

After all: As my friend Rabbi Stephen Landau has pointed out to me, without change we would die of boredom. Life would be unbearable. On a certain level we adore change. Change is what makes life *life*.

What changes will we be experiencing in the coming year? Which of these changes will be a result of our decisions and actions, and which will be beyond our control?

Every High Holidays we recite the following words in the Unetaneh Tokef prayer:

> On Rosh Hashanah it is written, on Yom Kippur it is sealed –
> How many shall pass on, how many shall come to be;
> Who shall live and who shall die;
> Who shall see ripe age and who shall not;
> Who shall perish by fire and who by water;
> Who by sword and who by beast;
> Who by hunger and who by thirst;
> Who by earthquake and who by plague;
> Who by strangling and who by stoning.

How do we understand these words? Do we take them literally? Do we believe that there is a heavenly book in which our names are written? And that this is the week in which our fates are recorded and sealed? Or do we reject that literalism as a primitive expression of fatalism?

I don't think we have to go in either of those directions. I think we can hear this passage as a poetic expression of our ancestors' and our own deep uncertainty: *We just don't know what will become of us this year.*

And it is also an expression of our even deeper knowing, because we *do* know what will become of us all eventually.

I was reviewing this Unetaneh Tokef prayer with a colleague recently, and we noticed something we don't recall noticing before. We had always assumed without much thought that the entire list of "Who shall this" and "Who shall that" is a catalog of all the different ways that a person might die. (And if you are familiar with the powerful Leonard Cohen song, "Who By Fire," it certainly seems to be a catalog of all the different ways that a person might die.) But upon closer look, we see that there are several lines that are not about that at all. There is a shift that happens partway through the list; and the pivotal point is "Who by strangling and who by stoning."

I always find this line the most difficult to recite out loud. It sounds so gruesome. And then I remembered recently – strangling and stoning were ancient rabbinic methods of capital punishment. (Whether they were ever actually implemented is debatable; but they were definitely discussed in great detail in the Talmud.) So these are two types of death that would be a consequence of one's own actions, rather than random occurrences out of one's control such as an earthquake or plague. If you had done something terribly wrong, this is how you would die. In other words, strangling and stoning don't fit with the previous lines of the prayer.

And with that, there is a shift to:

Who will rest and who will wander,
who will be harmonious and who will be harried,
who will enjoy tranquility and who will suffer,
who will be impoverished and who will be
enriched,
who will be degraded and who will be exalted.

These lines refer to ways of *living,* not ways of dying!
Ways of living which, one might argue, are at least in
part a result of our actions and the choices we make.

And finally, in the concluding line of the prayer, we
proclaim that turning our lives around, praying, and
acting righteously will "avert the severity of the
decree." Again, this image of a divine decree need not
be taken literally. The point is that we are not helpless
puppets in a divine drama. Our actions have consequences, and make a difference in the quality of our
lives and the lives of those we touch, for as long as we
remain alive.

Pirkei Avot, the collection of ethical teachings from
the early rabbis, expresses the paradox of the Unetaneh
Tokef prayer in one mind-bending line: "All is
foreseen, and freedom of choice is given." Do we have
control or don't we? The Jewish answer is: Yes, and
yes.

Besides these classic rabbinic teachings, the notion of
living in paradox is also expressed within kabbalah,
our mystical tradition. I have spoken on other
occasions about the kabbalistic tree of life, which can
be understood as a sort of psycho-spiritual map of
divine and human attributes. Mostly I have spoken
about the upper middle portion of the tree of life, in

which the attributes of Lovingkindness and Strict Judgment – Chesed and Gevurah – are portrayed as being in dynamic tension. The balancing of Loving-kindness and Strict Judgment leads to Tiferet, the quality of beauty and truth.

What is perhaps more relevant for this exploration of uncertainty, though, is the next lower pair of attributes in the tree: Netsach and Hod. The word Netsach may be translated as "endurance" or "success," and Hod is usually translated as "glory." Netsach represents courage, self-confidence, the belief in the possibility of big changes – the part of us that strides out into the world to make things *happen*. Hod represents acceptance, humility, gratitude, surrender, and silence. It is the part of us that knows the wisdom of letting go and letting be.

And, once again, the value is in seeking a balance between these two qualities. Living within the tension between what is and what could be. Living in the paradox.

The Unetaneh Tokef prayer expresses this dynamic tension between Netsach and Hod. So does the Pirkei Avot teaching. Yes, we are in control; and Yes, we are not in control.

Gam zeh ya'avor – This too shall pass – would seem to be an expression of Hod. It is a wise perspective on life, but our tradition encourages us not to stay in that perspective. Seeking the dynamic balance of Netsach and Hod, we might say: This too shall pass... and meanwhile, what am I going to *do*?

According to our mystical tradition, it is in the

dynamic balancing of these two attributes that the Tsaddik, the righteous person, is created.

May we all be blessed in this year 5772 with a healthy balancing of Netsach and Hod. May we develop the capacity to discern when to stride boldly out into the world, and when to sit quietly.

כן יהי רצון / *So may it be.*

Deep Trust

Yom Kippur 2011

On March 11th of this year, Japan was rocked by a massive earthquake followed by a terrifying tsunami. Imagine: One day you are going about your life, with a reasonable sense of certainty about what is happening and what will be happening... and the next day, everything you hold dear is literally swept away.

Everything about life is uncertain, except the certainty of change. Every one of us will be hit by a tsunami or a hurricane or some equally powerful blast in our lifetime. It's coming – for some of you, it may have already hit.

Everything about life is uncertain, except the certainty of change.

And yet... in our everyday lives, we act as if many things are certain, don't we? For example, we assume that the sun will rise every morning. Or, to be more accurate I should say: We assume that the earth is continuing to rotate at a certain pace as it orbits the sun. This is an example of what we might call the "mechanics" of nature that we take for granted and are largely unaware of. And we are unaware that we are unaware.

Stepping forward, we assume – unconsciously – that gravity will keep us standing on the ground. Throwing an object, we assume that it will follow the typical trajectory of objects being thrown. Do x, and the result will be y. We know these things from experience. For all practical purposes, we could say that we have certainty about them. And because we have certainty about them, we don't tend to have anxiety about them.

There is a midrash – a rabbinic tale – about Adam and Eve, the first human beings, and about their existential terror when the sun began to set on that very first day on earth. They had no idea that the sun would rise again the next morning, and assumed as it began to get cold and dark that their brief lives were coming to a dismal end. Sometimes young children experience anxieties like this, when they encounter some aspect of nature for the first time and do not know what adults have come to know and take for granted. With experience, though, we grow to take such things for granted.

But when it comes to anything other than the mechanics of nature, we really do not have certainty, (although we may pretend otherwise). In particular, when it comes to the things in our lives that matter most to us – relationships, health, livelihood – life is fraught with uncertainty.

Which brings us, on this holy day of Yom Kippur, to the question of faith.

Many modern Jews are not accustomed to talking about faith. The whole topic makes some of us uncomfortable. Perhaps slightly embarrassed. Faith? Isn't that a fundamentalist thing? A "bible belt" thing?

Some of you may recall my saying on other occasions that Judaism is not about what you *believe*, but about what you *do*. Am I contradicting myself now, saying that we need to talk about faith?

I don't think this is a contradiction. The kind of faith I want to talk about is not about belief in the typical sense of the word, as in the belief in things that cannot be proven. If we were talking about the belief in things that cannot be proven, then I would still say that Judaism is not about belief – not that sort of belief. For example: Do I believe that the Torah was physically handed down to Moses by God on Mount Sinai? Whether I do or not, is irrelevant. Judaism does not require that I believe it – Judaism requires that I act righteously, regardless of what I do or do not believe. Does a Jew need to believe in God to be a "good Jew"? I think the question is irrelevant. We can believe whatever we want to believe; what matters is how we behave.

Having said that, I want to talk about faith because I am a pragmatist. I want to talk about faith because we need it. That tsunami is coming, and we are each going to need all the help we can get. This is not an abstract, philosophical musing – this is very real.

What is a faith we can count on? What is a faith that goes beyond the literal, fundamentalist claims that many of us find so offensive to our sense of reason?

Here is a simple way of thinking about faith that I have found helpful: *Faith is deep trust*. Faith is a resting of the heart on something or someone – or upon Existence itself. It is no accident that the English word "believe" is so similar to the Hebrew word ba-lev, meaning "in – or upon – the heart." Faith is a matter of the heart, where categories of rational or irrational do not apply.

I am making a distinction here between believing and faith-ing, for lack of a better verb. Faith-ing is something that everyone does, regardless of whether you say "I believe in God" or not. In fact, faith is not necessarily about God at all. (And remember, as I said last year to those of you who say you don't believe in God: The God that you don't believe in, I don't believe in either!) So even if you would label yourself an atheist, you are still faith-ing! It is something that humans do; so this applies to everyone here.

One might say that we have faith in gravity, for example, in the sense that we have a deep trust – based on experience – that gravity will be there for us. We have an abiding trust that the sun will rise tomorrow morning, even though many of us cannot understand the physics behind it – again based on experience. Some of us have a profound trust in the power of love, based on experience.

Ultimately what we should be seeking is a faith grounded in experience, a faith that can be a source of courage and strength in the face of uncertainty.

Listen: That tsunami is coming. Will our faith sustain us, or will it shatter? I am reminded of one of my favorite lines in Psalms: "Esah aynei el he-harim, may-ayin yavo ezri – I lift up my eyes to the mountains, from where will my help come?" From where will our help come when that tsunami hits?

It may be that our faith will sustain us through a crisis or a tragedy. Or it may be that our faith will shatter under pressure.... And we can only hope that out of that shattering, a deeper and more trust-worthy faith will arise to replace it.

What will be the nature of the faith that will be your life-line when that tsunami hits? No one else can answer that question for you; but Judaism can help you to ask it.

Judaism offers spiritual tools to help us cultivate a trusting heart. Faith develops out of a life-long process of orienting the heart in this way. It is not about rationally choosing a philosophy because it sounds good, (although that doesn't hurt); it is about doing the spiritual work which will give us the lived experiences upon which to base our trust.

One of the primary spiritual tools in Judaism is the cultivation of humility. Moses, the all-time biggest hero in Jewish tradition, is revered for being – in the words of the Torah – the humblest man on the face of the earth. When his authority is challenged, he doesn't put up his dukes – he falls to the ground. He lowers his face to the ground. Not in the sense of giving up, but rather in the sense of acknowledging that this is not about his Ego.

In kabbalah, our mystical tradition, the goal of one's spiritual practice is sometimes referred to as the "nullification of the ego." Becoming Nothing rather than Something; and in so doing, becoming One with all that is. To use the Hebrew terms, becoming Ayin rather than Yesh. This leads to a fascinating word-play on the verse from Psalms I mentioned before. Esah aynei el he-harim, may-ayin yavo ezri is usually translated as "I lift up my eyes to the mountains, from where will my help come?" The word may-ayin means "from where." But may-ayin can also be translated as "from Ayin" – that is, from Nothing. With that twist, the verse is no longer a question, and may be interpreted this way: My help comes from Ayin, from the place where the Ego is dropped, from the place where we stop striving to be such a big Somebody. Or, in the words of our Buddhist friends: no Self, no problem.

So the cultivation of humility is one path to an enduring faith. Another path is referred to as "tsa-akah," crying out.

At the conclusion of the Unetaneh Tokef prayer, in which we recite "who shall live and who shall die, etc," we chant: "u-t'shuvah, u-t'filah, u-tsedakah ma'avirin et ro-ah ha-gezerah," translated in our prayerbooks as "But repentance, prayer, and charity temper judgment's severe decree." As I mentioned last night, this image of a divine decree need not be taken literally. The point is that we are not helpless puppets in a divine drama. Our actions have consequences, and make a difference in the quality of our lives and the lives of those we touch.

It happens that there are other statements in our tradition – in the Talmud, for example – suggesting what we can do to change our destiny. These other strategies include changing our name, changing our place, and *tsa-akah*, "crying out."

I do not believe that our sages meant "crying out" in the sense of what I call Vending Machine Theology. Prayers are not coins to be dropped into the cosmic vending machine in exchange for divinely served outcomes of *our* choosing. Please God, I want a flat-screen tv. Or even: Please God, my uncle needs a new kidney. Rather, Jewish tradition understands that the very process of pouring out our hearts – whether we call it crying out or praying – has a mysteriously transformative value, in and of itself.

And so we need to find ways to cry out. Ways to pray that go beyond the rote recitation of words that hold little meaning for us. And ways to discover – or re-discover – that those words in our prayerbook are the poetic expressions of our ancestors' efforts to cry out, to pour their hearts out.

A third spiritual path offered by Judaism is the path of *hakarat ha-tov*, or recognizing the good.

When I first sought input from all of you on the subject of uncertainty, someone responded to me that it's all about choices. I want to turn to that idea now. The path of recognizing the good is a choice we have in every moment. It is related to the path of gratitude, one of my personal favorites. It is the path that teaches us to recite at least 100 *brachot* – 100 blessings – a day in appreciation for the wonders of life. It is the path that teaches us to say *gam zu l'tovah*, "this too is for the good," even in the face of a situation that hardly seems good on the surface. It is the path that teaches us, in the words of today's Torah reading, to "choose life."

In the face of uncertainty, we always have a choice. We can choose hope and courage over fear. We can choose generosity of spirit over anxiety. This is not about being a Pollyanna. This is about cultivating a deep trust based on experience. The more we live from a place of *hakarat ha-tov*/recognizing the good, the more that goodness becomes our life experience… and the more we can trust it. In this I have faith.

The Intention to Forgive

Erev Rosh Hashanah 2012

Sometimes when I'm driving, the thought arises: How awesome it is – in the old-fashioned, trembling sense of the word – awesome, that my life could be forever altered in a *snap*. Not only that my life could end suddenly – which is certainly always a possibility – but that I could – in one careless moment – be the cause of someone else's injury or death.

And I wonder how I would ever, ever live with myself if that happened. And I imagine that I would never be the same again.

A similar thought, which arises less often but is equally awe-inducing: My life could be forever altered in a *snap* by someone else's act of violence.

I find that I have trouble saying such things out loud without murmuring a quick "kinahora," as if it were possible to ward off the possibility of pain and death with a little Yiddish. But this is an awesome season in our calendar, and I want to face the awesome truth with at least a bit less fear.

These thoughts came to mind again recently, when I read the story of Kelly Connor. Kelly Connor is a 58-year-old woman who, while driving at the age of 17, struck and killed an elderly woman in a pedestrian crossing. Kelly Connor's story of decades of inner torment, and eventual, tentative self-forgiveness, is one of over 100 powerful stories featured on the website of the Forgiveness Project.

The Forgiveness Project is an organization which collects and shares real stories of forgiveness and reconciliation, personal testimonies of both victims and perpetrators of crime and violence around the world. These are not easy stories to read. Kelly Connor's story was the easiest to read, because at least her crime was not intentional. These are dreadful stories that you might hear about on the news, but with a twist – they are personal testimonies not simply of pain endured, but of valiant efforts to keep the heart open despite unbearable torment.

To read these stories is awesome – in the old-fashioned, trembling sense of the word. As I read one after the other, I knew that I had to tell you about them, because these stories ultimately convey such a profound message of *hope*. And hope is, after all, what the celebration of a new year is all about.

For several years I have wanted to speak about forgiveness on the high holidays. It is a central theme of the traditional liturgy, after all. But I never felt like I had the moral authority to do it. Never felt like I had any more of a handle on forgiveness than anyone else. Who has the chutzpah to exhort anyone else to seek, or to bestow, forgiveness? I dreaded sounding hypocritically pious.

Finding the Forgiveness Project felt like a partial answer to my dilemma. There are *stories* to be heard, and learned from, and inspired by. Personal stories shared by ordinary people. Stories from Rwanda, and Sarajevo. Stories from Ireland, and Israel, and

Palestine. And stories closer to home as well. Probably some of us have experienced, or personally know of, similar stories of forgiveness, enough to fill a book.

The Forgiveness Project stories are not feel-good, Pollyanna stories. Blood has been spilled. Lives have been shattered. The stories of what these people have experienced – both the victims and the perpetrators – push *us* to the limits of what we can even bear to hear, let along imagine experiencing. And that they have been able to transform their unbearable pain into something decent and honorable should be a source of inspiration to us.

These are not stories with simplistic happy endings. In addition to the burdens of memory these people will carry forever, many of them – both the perpetrators and the victims – continue to face condemnation from others for their efforts to seek forgiveness and reconciliation. They are criticized and even demonized, sometimes by family members or former friends. Their actions – and the actions of their critics – push *us* to the limits of our understanding and acceptance of the full spectrum of human nature.

Think for a moment. Aren't there some scenarios of crime or violence for which your gut reaction would be that forgiveness is unthinkable, perhaps even obscene? And yet, ordinary people like you and me continue to reach for the possibility of peace of mind which forgiveness and/or reconciliation can bring out of even the most horrific experiences.

Remember: Forgiveness does not wipe away the deed. Forgiveness does not mean forgetting, or excusing what was done. But forgiveness can take the forgiver to a better place within themselves.

When I asked over the summer for input from temple members for my high holiday sermons, one member wrote the following:

> Although there are prayers for peace, I think, particularly in these times, it is important to have peace of mind. Whether that be peace from job (therefore money) worries, or peace of mind relative to these horrible mass shootings, or from the threat of foreign terrorists when we go traveling or to large venues. And, particularly, for those of us who have young children and/or grandchildren, some kind of peace for their generation.

To this I say "amen." And, this begs the question: *How* is peace of mind to be attained?

Putting aside how we might answer that question in relation to the victims and perpetrators of crimes and violence…. For those of us who have not had that particular experience – kinahora – let's consider instead the hurts we experience and inflict on one another every day.

In the words of meditation teacher Jack Kornfield, who himself suffered terribly as a child at the hands of an abusive, chaotic father:

> There are many ways that we have hurt and harmed others, have betrayed or abandoned them, caused them suffering, knowingly or unknowingly, out of our pain, fear, anger, and confusion….

Just as we have caused suffering to others, there are many ways that we have hurt and harmed ourselves. We have betrayed or abandoned ourselves many times in thought, word, or deed, knowingly or unknowingly....

[And] there are many ways... others have hurt, wounded, or harmed us, out of fear, pain, confusion, and anger; ...knowingly or unknowingly, in thought, word, or deed.*

The 10 days between Rosh Hashanah and Yom Kippur are traditionally referred to as *Aseret Y'mai Teshuvah*, the ten days of teshuvah. The Hebrew word teshuvah is usually translated as "repentance," but that's not quite it. The root meaning of the word teshuvah has to do with *turning*, and with *responding*.

So we turn to look at ourselves, we turn away from our mistakes, we turn back towards our ideals, we re-turn to our best selves, we respond to our past actions with new ideas, we turn to apologize to people we have wronged.

You can understand this turning and responding in so many ways. Through honest and compassionate self-reflection, we re-orient ourselves back onto the path towards peace of mind.

Many people know that this is the traditional season for teshuvah, but it is less well known that in Judaism, teshuvah is meant to be an on-going, *daily* practice. In answer to the question "How is peace of mind to be attained?," our tradition offers this life long practice (among many others).

Think about it. What might your life be like if every evening – or even just once a week – you paused to recollect the ways you have hurt others, the ways you have hurt yourself, and the ways others have hurt you... and with each recollection, you lifted up an intention to *forgive*? An intention to keep the heart open?

I encourage you to experiment with a regular practice of forgiveness. And may this be the year that we drop the burdens of anger and resentment we carry, and open our hearts to greater love and compassion and healing.

כן יהי רצון / *So may it be.*

---

* *The Art of Forgiveness, Lovingkindness, and Peace,* Jack Kornfield, Bantam Books 2012

A Radical Understanding of Prayer

Rosh Hashanah 2012

A story: Some years ago there was a car crash in front of the Baptist church in the town where my family used to live. The driver, taking her eyes off the road to turn and yell at her children in the back seat, swerved and hit an on-coming vehicle. The children were injured, the older girl critically. The Baptist church undertook a 'round-the-clock prayer vigil. When at last the girl was released from the hospital, a member of the church wrote a letter to the local newspaper congratulating the church for the power of its prayers, taking credit for the girl's survival.

Another story: I met a woman who was visiting her critically ill friend in the hospital. She was distraught because the medical staff would not discuss her friend's condition with her and tell her which organs and systems of the body were malfunctioning. She said to me: "How can I pray if I don't know specifically what I'm praying for? I need to know what I'm praying for."

Two years ago on Yom Kippur, I offered a radical perspective on God which opened up a lot of conversation and reflection for quite some time afterwards. People are still reading that sermon on the internet, two years later.

Today I want to take the next step, and share a radical approach to prayer. Why? Because I think we've gotten boxed into a corner that is not a very Jewish corner. And because there is a lot of suffering in our lives, and this could help.

The corner we have gotten boxed into is *the assumption that prayer is a means to gain a desired outcome from God.* You may believe it, you may reject it – but either way, you are still in the same tight corner if you assume that's what prayer is.

I hope to persuade you today that there is a radical alternative to this understanding of prayer – an alternative for those of you who believe in prayer, and an alternative for those of you who reject it. An alternative that is both traditional and practical... and potentially transformational.

First a brief refresher course on God. Here is what I shared with you two years ago:

> The God that you don't believe in, I don't believe in either.
>
> The God that many of you don't believe in is the biblical, personal God. This is the God who *does* things, who listens and responds, who is sort of like a very large, very powerful invisible *person,* only somehow more so. It is the God who speaks from a burning bush, the God who splits the sea so the Israelites can walk through on dry ground, the God who answers (or perversely doesn't answer) personal prayers... the God who should have saved us from the Holocaust but didn't. It is the God that doesn't make logical sense to a thoughtful older

child, and is therefore so often rejected as "not existing" by the time of bat or bar mitzvah. It is the God that leads many thoughtful people like you to conclude that religion is naïve, and that only science can be trusted as a map of reality.

A perfect articulation of this common experience – from Ira Glass, host of Chicago Public Radio's *This American Life*. Ira Glass said in a recent interview in the *Forward* newspaper: "The notion that there is a big supernatural daddy in the sky, pushing the chess pieces around, came to seem unrealistic to me... [In Hebrew school] I'd already decided I didn't believe in God, and am now pretty much a nonpracticing, nonbelieving, cultural Jew."

In my Yom Kippur sermon two years ago, I went on to share a radical, alternative understanding of God based in Jewish tradition: God is the name we give to the totality of existence. God is Reality with a capital R, unfathomable, mysterious. God is not a being, God is Being with a capital B. God – or rather, yud-hey-vav-hey, or Adonai – is the name we give to the unity underlying all of existence. When we say Shema Yisrael Adonai eloheinu *Adonai echad*, it's not so much that we are saying there is only one God, but we are declaring that God is One – there is nothing else. We, and everything else in existence, are temporary manifestations of God, all part of the One.

It seemed that many of you found this alternative understanding of God liberating and helpful. So now let's liberate prayer:

If we believe that God is a "big supernatural daddy in

the sky, pushing the chess pieces around," then prayer is our attempt to *influence* God. To put it somewhat crudely: We praise and thank God to get on God's good side, and then we ask for what we want. Human beings have been doing some version of this since pre-historic times.

And if we believe that prayer is a means to influence this personal God to give us a desired outcome, then our prayer is either "answered" or "not answered." If our desired outcome does not come about, we either say our prayer was not answered because of some failure on our part, or we say God "knows better" or "has a different plan" or "works in mysterious ways" – all of which are still assuming that God is a very large, very powerful invisible person up there somewhere, who is listening and responding (or not), and ultimately in control.

Another variation on this theme – Some people will say that they don't believe in a personal God *per se*, but they pray to the Universe, or to "Source," or some other term which still suggests some ultimate power that can grant us what we ask for. And again, when those prayers are not "answered," a believer will conclude that it is either due to some failure on their part, or the incomprehensible workings of that invisible power.

And then there are those of you I know who have concluded that prayer simply does not make sense. God is not a person or being or entity to be influenced, and therefore prayers for specific desired outcomes are irrational and even offensive.

Here is one obvious, rational argument against prayer to a personal God: In the same week that those earnest Baptists I mentioned earlier were praying for that little girl in the car crash, millions of mothers' voices were raised in prayer around the world for their critically ill children – and millions of those children died that week. What kind of a perverse deity answers prayers for some children but not others?

Is it any wonder that so many people have walked away from prayer – indeed from religion itself? This assumption about prayer has boxed us into a tight corner.

Listen – If prayer is a means to gain a desired outcome from a supernatural God, then we just can't win... . because what we really desire – *what we really desire* – is to live without pain, to live without loss, and to live without dying... and there is no God who can satisfy those desires.

As I have said before, I do not believe in the biblical, personal God. And by extension, I do not believe that prayers are either "answered" or "not answered." If it is possible to understand God differently, then let us consider the possibility that prayer also can be something other than what we have been assuming.

So let us at last set aside the assumption that prayer is a means to gain a desired outcome from a supernatural God. If it's not about that, then what is it? And why pray?

Consider for a moment: Why are we here today? Why

are each of you here? I imagine that we are here for a variety of reasons. And I am willing to bet that underlying every reason, there is some sense of *longing* in all of our hearts.

That longing – that deep sense of yearning – is the "religious" impulse in human nature, and we should not minimize it or push it aside in our everyday life just because we conclude that it is irrational.

An analogy: Music and art – the creation and enjoyment of beauty – are fundamental aspects of the human experience. When we push them aside as irrational or unnecessary, we cripple our souls. The religious impulse is likewise a fundamental aspect of the human experience.

Some of you have heard me say before that the essence of Jewish prayer can be distilled into three words: Wow! Thanks! Please!

Wow, thanks, please. Beyond being a handy classification system for *all* the prayers in our vast liturgy, these three words provide us with the spiritual template we need.

How does this differ from what I mentioned earlier, our pre-historic habit of praising and thanking God to get on God's good side, and then asking for what we want? The difference comes down to how we understand the "please."

Wow is the expression of awe and humility. Thanks is the expression of gratitude. Wow and Thanks alone give us a lifetime of spiritual work, and don't require a belief in a personal God. So what's up with the "please"?

We have a tradition in Judaism that prayer is a pouring out of the heart.... but not for the purpose of influencing God to give us what we want. We pour out our heart because we need to. We pour out our heart because of its effect on our soul. We pour out our heart because in doing so we become more self-aware. It is a spiritual practice.

The source for the practice of pouring out your heart in prayer can be found in today's haftarah reading from the first book of Samuel: A woman named Channah is praying at the holy temple, and the high priest Ayli is watching her. Though her lips are moving, Channah makes no sound that can be heard from a distance, so that Ayli thinks she is drunk and chastises her for it. Channah replies that she has had no liquor, but has been pouring out her heart before the Lord, out of her sorrow and grief. She says *Eshpoch et nafshi lifnai Adonai* – literally, I poured out my soul, my life-force – my *nefesh* – in the presence of God.

The story goes on to say, as ancient biblical stories often do, that Hannah's prayer for a son was soon answered... which to me is not the point of the story! What is more significant is that the rabbis who came along later saw in this story a prototype for personal prayer. This is one of many of the spiritual practices known as *tefillah* (the Hebrew word for prayer).

We too can develop a regular tefillah practice of pouring out our soul. It's not difficult to do. Alone or in a group – in nature, or in our home, or here during services – we can set aside some time to whisper whatever is on our minds or in our hearts. Note that it is the *vocalizing* of our words that is of particular benefit in this practice. This is *not* about prayer within the structure of the prayer book. This is about a personal tefillah practice, in which you do not need to know Hebrew nor be familiar with the traditional written prayers.

So, advice for the new year: Try developing a personal tefillah practice. Daily, weekly, whatever works for you. Two minutes, twenty minutes, whatever works for you. Don't wait to pray until there is a crisis or when someone you love is ill.

In his book *Making Prayer Real*, Rabbi Mike Comins writes: "In its essence, prayer is the practice of becoming more aware and more compassionate. It is a way of speaking truth and opening the heart." That's it. That's the practice of tefillah.

One last thing: In a recent book entitled *Search Inside Yourself*, one of Google's founding engineers shares a simple program of mindfulness practice that has been life-transforming for Google employees and that they intend to share with the world. One of the recommended practices has all the elements of this tefillah practice I am suggesting. The goal of Google's program is greater self-awareness, and the book offers ample scientific evidence that greater self-awareness leads to greater compassion and greater happiness. So don't just take it from me and the ancient rabbis. Take it from Google: A prayer practice is good for you.

כן יהי רצון / *So may it be.*

Cultivating Empathy and Compassion

Kol Nidrei 2012

Yom Kippur is a paradox, and I love paradoxes.

As the 20th century physicist Neils Bohr once said, "How wonderful that we have met with a paradox. Now we have some hope of making progress."

On the one hand, Yom Kippur is all about what we've done wrong. About our short-comings, our screw-ups, our failures. Look at us: What have we done in our lives so far? According to the mahzor, we have been arrogant, bigoted, deceitful, greedy, unjust, malicious, and much, much more. The message is that we really need to get our act together and turn things around before it's too late.

On the other hand, Yom Kippur is inevitably about the joy of being alive. About hope, and the possibility of waking up. Look at us: What have we done in our lives so far? We have been compassionate, gracious, patient, loving and truthful. In the Yom Kippur liturgy we ascribe these qualities to God, which is another way of saying how highly we value those qualities in ourselves and others.

Why does there seem to be such an emphasis in the Yom Kippur mahzor on our wrong-doing, sins, transgressions, or "missing of the mark"? Here is one answer: Perfection is a divine attribute – not a human one.

We are not expected to be perfect. We are expected to keep striving towards great self-awareness in our daily lives, and to thereby minimize the hurt we cause ourselves and others. The more self-aware we are, the less we will speak and act from a place of anger, greed, or fear.

And we are human, which means that inevitably we will speak and act from a place of anger, greed, or fear. So then what?

The liturgy of Yom Kippur points us towards the healing process of teshuvah and forgiveness. Hopefully teshuvah and forgiveness are part of our lives daily or weekly; but if not, Yom Kippur comes once a year to clear away the accumulated shmutz of our unskillful words and actions during the past year, revealing once again our radiant, child-like goodness.

The Hebrew root word *chaper*, from which *kippur* is derived, is usually translated as atonement but also carries the meaning of "to scrub." The ancient high priest scrubbed down the "holy of holies" in the sanctuary of the temple in Jerusalem in preparation for Yom Kippur. The rabbis later imagined that each of us experiences an analogous, spiritual scrub-down in our inner "holy of holies" on Yom Kippur. The gift of it – the grace, if you will – is that it's automatic. The Talmud tells us that the day of Yom Kippur itself does the atoning.

This is a provocative idea. I invite you to set aside your skepticism and the intellectual detachment that our culture breeds in us. Let yourself experience that this is real for you now, today. That you are deserving of forgiveness and a fresh start. That the day of Yom Kippur is somehow, inexplicably, giving your soul a scrubbing that will restore its original purity.

Now, this gift of a refurbished soul on Yom Kippur does not mean that we can walk away from the very real messes we have made on this earthly plane! Jewish tradition is clear about that. In a recent chat, an old friend of mine put it this way: "People need to acknowledge what they've done and know that they can do it differently. Do what you can to make amends – apologize, admit guilt, express concern, pay someone back, return something, whatever. And then, move on."

This year it seems to me that Yom Kippur is more other-directed than it is self-directed. It is not about personal growth, or at least not about personal growth as an end in itself. All this self-reflection on Yom Kippur is designed to point us in the direction of greater compassion, empathy, and *action* on behalf of others.

There are at least two places in the mahzor where this comes through loud and clear. First is in the vidui/confession, when we recite the litany of transgressions not as "I" but as "we." Phillip Birnbaum, the editor of a well-known edition of the mahzor in the 1950s, explained it this way: "The confession is phrased in the plural because it is made collectively by the whole community regarding itself responsible for many offenses that could have been prevented." That is a challenging statement.

Here is another interpretation of the practice, from the 16th century kabbalist Isaac Luria: "Why was the confession composed in the plural, so that we say We have sinned, rather than, I have sinned? Because all Israel is one body and every one of Israel is a limb of that body; that is why we are all responsible for one another when we sin. So, if one's fellow should sin, it is as though one has sinned oneself; therefore, despite the fact that one has not committed that iniquity, one must confess to it. For when one's fellow has sinned, it is as though one has sinned oneself."

What Luria is referring to is the belief that *kol Yisrael arevim zeh la-zeh* / all Jews are responsible for one another. (You might want to expand the expression to include all people, not just Jews, depending where you happen to be at the moment on the universalism vs. particularism spectrum.) The Hebrew root word *arev* means responsible for; it also means mixed up with. We are all mixed up in this together, this wild adventure called living.

The second place in the mahzor where this message of compassionate action comes through is in the haftarah from the book of Isaiah which we will read tomorrow. The people are complaining that their day of fasting did not bring them the material bounty they had bargained for. The prophet Isaiah thunders in response:

> Is that what you call fasting, a day acceptable to the Lord?
> Behold, this is the fast that I esteem precious:
> Loosen the chains of wickedness, undo the bonds of oppression,

Let the crushed go free, break all yokes of tyranny!
Share your food with the hungry, take the poor to
your home,
Clothe the naked when you see them, never turn
from your fellow.
Then shall your light dawn, your healing shall
come soon;
Your triumph shall go before you, the Lord's glory
backing you....

Isaiah's words continue to challenge us.

One final thought on the cultivation of empathy and
compassion on Yom Kippur, and the interplay
between the personal and the communal:

If we can get a sense that we are worthy of forgiveness, then we can realize that other people are too.
If we have wronged someone and thereby been the
cause of their suffering, and if we have suffered
remorse because of it, then we can empathize with
others in a similar situation. Through our own
suffering we can come to know the suffering of others,
and know that they too are in need not only of
forgiveness but also of help. As the Baal Shem Tov
has suggested, by our own pain we know what the
world needs.

So may it be that on this Yom Kippur we experience
not only a deep sense of forgiveness and healing for
ourselves, but also a renewed sense of compassionate
obligation to care for others.

כן יהי רצון / *So may it be.*

Love and Loss

Yom Kippur 2012

Dear God,

I am writing to You on behalf of my congregation. Although we have differences of opinion about You, and some of us are uncertain about what "believing in You" means, we still feel the impulse to communicate with You occasionally. To address the awesome mystery of existence as "You." We can't seem to help it sometimes.

Anyway, I am writing this letter to You on behalf of my congregation on the subject of love and loss. There has been much personal loss in this little congregation, and it is on our minds. I promise, God, not to ask "Why?" or at least not to ask it too often. I know that asking "why" questions puts a person on the defensive. Of course You are not a person, but still I know that asking why You, God, do this or that is not a fruitful line of inquiry, because there is never a satisfactory answer.

Ribono shel Olam / Master of the universe: Everything we love, we will eventually lose. Everything, and everyone. This is the truth of being human. We get that – intellectually, sometimes – and yet we are thrown by it over and over. A trivial first example: that delicious pasta the other night, with the fresh sautéed mushrooms and garlic. I loved it, and then it was gone. There is the joy in the experience, and then the flash of sadness at the loss of that experience. And for some reason, You set life up to be this way.

Okay God, You know I'm not complaining about the loss of a great pasta dinner. It's not like I really wanted it to last forever, God forbid. But You know what I mean. Every moment, every breath, every experience... comes to us, and then it's gone. Loss is built into the system of existence at its core. As long as we exist in time, everything has a beginning and an end. And every time we wish it were otherwise, we suffer.

I imagine that from Your perspective, God, it's not loss at all. It's just change. The human twist is to perceive change as loss, and to suffer because of it. Why have our minds evolved to be like this? I'm just wondering, God, I'm not expecting an answer.

Maybe, being God, You don't understand what I mean by love and loss. So maybe it would be helpful for You to know how it seems from our side:

Throughout our lives, not just on the moment-to-moment level that I mentioned before, but year after year, we experience losses. Precious objects, precious people, precious beliefs and understandings. Beginning in childhood with the loss of a beloved pet, the loss of a revered hero, the loss of a friend who moves away, the loss of a grandparent – or even, God forbid, a parent or sibling, – the first shock of betrayal by a trusted friend, the shame of being ridiculed by someone we adore. Childhood losses may seem trivial from Your grand universal perspective, but each loss can cause suffering that is far from trivial to us.

I still remember the day when I lost faith in the perfection of grownups. (Likely there were other days too, but this one I remember clearly.) I was in the third grade – 45 years ago – , and my beloved teacher Mrs. Lefkowitz (of blessed memory) was telling us about a woman she knew who had eaten so many carrots that her skin took on an orange tint. This story struck me as preposterous, and for the first time the thought arose in my 8-year-old mind that my beloved Mrs. Lefkowitz was either wrong or lying to us. Either possibility was devastating. And in that moment, something was lost. I was never the same (even after learning years later that her story was not preposterous at all).

Loss is a natural part of life. It is inevitable. We get that – intellectually, sometimes – but then we forget again. Our ancestors shared with us a few stories, with You as a central character, apparently trying to find ways to remember this truth too. Like the one where You created the world, and there were Adam and Eve, living the good life, and then BAM – they became human and they lost paradise. That story reminds us that loss is inevitable if you are human.

It also raises the question of how we *respond* to the pain of loss. Eve eats the fruit, Adam eats the fruit, You call Adam out for disobeying, and Adam responds… "*She* made me do it." The first story in the Torah of loss in a human relationship, the first instance of blame.

It seems like we do that a lot, God. We experience loss, and we rush to deflect our pain. Blame, busyness, anger, sarcasm, humor, addiction – various strategies You have given us for avoiding acceptance of the reality of loss.

When I asked for input from temple members on this theme, one person wrote to me: "So often blessings are mixed with sadness and loss." Ribono shel Olam, I want to tell You two stories that relate to her comment. These stories were told to me by a man in his 80s (not a temple member). I'll call him Joseph.

Story number one: As a young father, Joseph would arrive home from work every day, park the car, and walk along a sidewalk that passed a little neighborhood playground in front of his home. His daughter always played there, and every day she would see him and come dashing down the sidewalk shouting "Daddy! Daddy!" and fly into his arms. It was the high point of each day for him.

One day he arrived home, parked the car, and walked along the sidewalk towards the playground. His daughter looked up, called out "Hi Daddy!" and went back to what she was doing.

Recalling this story for me 50 years later brought tears to his eyes. He can still remember the pain he felt in that moment.

And then he recalled another story: In his own childhood, in Brooklyn, his father had the custom of going for a walk in the neighborhood every evening after dinner. And every evening, Joseph accompanied his father on this walk. It was just something they did together. Sometimes they would talk, but mostly they just walked around the streets of Brooklyn.

One evening, when Joseph was 15, he was invited by a

friend to hang out with the guys in front of the candy store on the corner after dinner. He knew there would be girls there too. When dinner ended and his father signaled his readiness to go for a walk, Joseph told him about the invitation to join his friends, and he got up from the table and left. Later, his father stopped by the street corner where Joseph was hanging out, and said "so, are you coming for a walk now?" Joseph replied "Nah, I think I'll just stay here." His father's face fell – just for a moment – just long enough for Joseph to see a flash of sorrow in his father's eyes that no amount of apologizing could ever undo.

The two stories are really one story from Your perspective, aren't they, God? Children grow up and that is a wonderful blessing, and yet each developmental accomplishment for them is both a joy and a mini-death for their parents.

And then of course as we get older, we experience very real losses that are not tinged with joy. The loss of aspects of our identity, such as "wife" or "husband." The loss of employment. The loss of ease of movement or other physical abilities, or sight, or hearing. The loss of stamina. The loss of an old home. The loss of old friends, companions, family members. The loss of the familiar, the comfortable. From Your perspective, God, it's just more of the inevitable changes of life. For us, it can be one painful challenge after another.

I suppose Yours is the epitome of the Big Picture perspective. Here, we tend to be much more focused on our own little lives. And in our own little lives, as one member of the congregation said to me, "time flies and life changes before our eyes."

Psalm 90, a song written to You thousands of years ago, says the same thing: "You hurry us away, we vanish as suddenly as the grass. In the morning it shoots up and flourishes, in the evening it wilts and dies."

Yom Kippur itself is an annual reminder that really every moment, every exhalation, is a mini-death. Our tradition has many such built-in reminders. For example, the nightly meditation on forgiveness which I mentioned here on Erev Rosh Hashanah is called a vidui, a confession, similar to that which is to be recited on our deathbed. It seems that You have given us on-going opportunities to practice letting go. We are still not very graceful about it, though.

And then there is the Jewish people as a whole. Ribono shel Olam, it's a funny thing about us Jews. Somehow it has become part of our collective psyche to ritually recall our losses. Not for us the easy sleep of forgetfulness. We re-tell our losses annually. We immortalize our losses.

I know this isn't about You, God. It's really about us – how we try to create meaning out of our suffering. The rabbinic imagination created an entire system of sanctifying our memories, of making them central to our sense of identity as a people. Have You noticed that we make a big deal out of passing our memories on to the next generation (although some of us worry that we are not doing it well enough)? We seem to carry with us both a communal and a personal sense of longing – longing for something precious which is no more.

So what are we to do, given that everything we love, we will eventually lose? How shall we live?

I hear two answers. Two answers heard and shared by many people before us. Two answers most clearly expressed by two ancient voices in our tradition.

The first voice is that of the composer of Psalm 90, who sang with aching clarity of the brevity of our lives, and then gave us one of the most beautiful lines in scripture: "Therefore, teach us to number our days that we may get a heart of wisdom."

To number our days. In modern English we might say: Pay attention to the preciousness of every day.

The other voice is that of Kohelet, from the biblical book known as Ecclesiastes. After thoroughly examining all aspects of life and concluding that all is "mere breath," Kohelet bypasses existential despair by urging us to enjoy what we have while we have it: Find joy in loving relationships, do the work that you are able to do, have a few good friends, enjoy food and drink. *Experience joy.* "Until," Kohelet says, "the silver cord is snapped, and the golden bowl is smashed, and the pitcher is broken against the well, and the jug smashed at the pit. And dust returns to the earth as it was, and the life-breath returns to God who gave it."

Together, Kohelet and the psalmist remind us: Pay attention to the ordinary and find joy in it, *and* know that everything we love, we will eventually lose. This is the truth of being human.

I hear one more answer, this one from Your "still small voice" in my heart: Life is not only about "love and loss," but also – and perhaps more importantly – about "loss and love." As we experience loss, it is the love of family and friends that sustains us.

May we be blessed in the coming year with more love in our lives, more love to sustain us through our inevitable losses.

כן יהי רצון / *So may it be.*

Memory and Forgiveness

Erev Rosh Hashanah 2013

A kitchen table memory: I am eight years old. I am alone at the kitchen table, poking at the cold remains of dinner on my plate. My father and brother have already eaten and gone. My mother is at the sink doing dishes, her back to me. I have been told to sit alone for as long as it will take to finish the cold remains of dinner on my plate. I have been told that I am a "slow eater." I have been told that I talk too much during meals.

The brown formica-top kitchen table my parents purchased after their marriage in 1952, used as a kitchen table until my mother's death this past June, is now the work table in my home office. Inheriting this kitchen table and re-purposing it in our home is affecting me in ways I could not have imagined.

Memory and forgiveness.

Rosh Hashanah is called Yom ha-Zikaron, the day of remembrance. Today we are instructed to recall our memories. Today we are instructed to review our lives. Today we are instructed to look back at this past year and gauge how far we've come on our journey. There is a quality of judgment to this life review, yet also a quality of forgiveness. In the poetic metaphors of the High Holiday prayers, God is the judge and yet God is also the loving parent.

This is traditionally the season of forgiveness; but we cannot forgive what we cannot remember. And so we are instructed first to remember.

The Torah instructs the Israelite people repeatedly to remember. *Zachor*, the imperative, the command. Remember. But as the historian Yosef Yerushalmi points out, this ancient command is not a command that we all become historians. It is not a command to remember details and facts for their own sake. Rather, it is a command to remember and to pass on the *meaning* of events. This is what we as Jews are instructed to do.

What was the meaning our ancient ancestors passed on to the next generation when they remembered events in the life of the community? *God makes things happen for us*. This was what the Israelites were commanded to remember. Miracle? The hand of God. Redemption? The hand of God. Even the rising up of an enemy power? The hand of God. This is the ancient understanding embedded in the Torah.

If that theology doesn't work for us, we can understand the Torah's message another way. This is what we are commanded to remember: There is a bigger picture to the events of our lives. You can call it God if you need to, but the point is, there is always a larger context to what we are experiencing. We are but tiny manifestations of the mystery of existence as a whole.

The Torah's message was primarily intended for the tribe, not the individual, but I think it holds true for both. The Jewish people maintains a strong tradition of remembering mythic events and passing on their meaning; the primary example being the Exodus from Egypt retold annually at our Passover seders. Likewise we have the imperative to remember the events in our personal lives. We remember not merely for the sake of cataloging facts. We remember not just to feel victimized. We remember for the sake of *transformation*. What was the meaning of the event at the time it happened, and what is the transformative meaning that we are able to find or create in the act of remembering? It is not coincidental that the modern field of psychology, psychoanalysis in particular, has Jewish roots.

The act of remembering can be transformative. The first time I wrote down my kitchen table memory about sitting alone at the table after dinner when I was eight years old, the language I used was subtly different. I first wrote: "I was being forced to sit alone... I was being punished for being a slow eater... I was being punished for talking too much." And as I wrote, I could feel the heat of shame rising, and anger at having been treated unjustly.

Then I came back a few days later to what I had written, and questions began to arise. "Forced"? Really? It may have felt that way to me as a child, but it is more accurate to say "I was *told* to sit alone..." I could, in fact, have left the table at any time. There may have been unpleasant consequences, but I did have that choice.

And as for being "punished" – In retrospect, my parents may not have perceived their instructions as punishing. Or they may have perceived it as entirely justifiable punishment. This was, after all, a post-war American Jewish household in which eating all of what was on one's plate was simply what every child was expected to do. And there were also strong cultural norms around children's behavior at meal time and the necessity for being mostly "seen and not heard." So my energetic talking, coupled with my aversion to my mother's cooking, may simply have been *wrong* in the eyes of my young parents.

My young parents! What did they know about how to raise two children? What did anyone know? As a child I could not have known what they were going through at that time. But as an adult I can look at this story now with a wider view, can listen to this story now with a more nuanced ear. Can empathize now with all the people in this story with *rachmones*, a heart of compassion.

My mother, I learned over a decade later, suffered throughout my childhood with untreated depression, and my chatter at the end of the day may have felt like an unbearable assault on her nerves. How desperately she tried to be a proper suburban housewife, but just getting through the day must have at times over-whelmed her.

Another kitchen table memory: I am eleven years old. I am sitting at the table, eating an unusually large breakfast. Today is my Red Cross swim test at the JCC. My mother has prepared a special meal to give me extra energy, but my stomach is already tightening with anxiety about the swim test. Mom is sitting across from me, chatting with someone on the phone (which is attached to the wall with a long coiled cord). Suddenly I announce that I am *not* going to take the swim test after all. Instead of pausing her phone conversation to inquire about my decision and perhaps try to talk me out of it, she mouths "okay," and continues talking on the phone. I disappear up into my room.

As my b'nai mitzvah students are hopefully learning, Torah stories often seem simple until you look at them closely with the mindset of a detective. A deeper exploration is necessary to unearth meaning. Not *the* meaning, but *your* meaning.

I imagine that each of you has a family story that is highly emotionally charged for *you* but innocuous on the surface to anyone else. This kitchen table memory is one of those stories for me. You may be wondering, what's the big deal here? She ate breakfast, she changed her mind about something that was making her nervous, her mom said okay, she went upstairs. Where's the deep meaning in that? My point here is not to engage you in psychoanalyzing my childhood – but rather to suggest that with every memory recalled comes the possibility of transformation.

The more we look at a story, the more meaning we uncover. This is Torah study. This is what Jews do.

The traditional Torah reading for Rosh Hashanah is from a family story. The story of Abraham, Sarah, Hagar, Ishmael and Isaac is an epic story of love, jealousy, competition, abuse, anger, fear, hope, and redemption. In other words, it is our story. A temple member shared with me that one of the possible reasons given for why we read this story on Rosh Hashanah of all days is that it points us towards the deep task of forgiving our parents.

Memory and forgiveness. We can recall memories in order to re-open old wounds, or we can recall memories in order to transform them, and ourselves.

May this coming year be one in which we all find ways to recall those memories that are still in need of healing, and find redemptive meaning in them. May we remember in order to understand the bigger picture. May we remember in order to heal and forgive. May we remember and be transformed.

כן יהי רצון / *So may it be.*

This is How It Always Ends

Rosh Hashanah 2013

My father died nine years ago. Some years after he died, my mother emptied his Brooks Brothers pajamas out of the top drawer of his dresser to make space for a few of her things. Other than that, the dresser remained untouched. Mom eventually moved out of the house to an apartment in our hometown, and then two years ago moved up here to Sharon. My father's untouched dresser went with her for both moves. When my mother died this past June and I was faced with the task of clearing out her apartment, I began with my father's dresser. Among the treasures (and junk) I unearthed in that dresser was a large, obviously old, manila envelope.

Within the envelope I found a checkbook, a savings bank passbook, a bank statement, a high school report card, a high school diploma, a birth certificate, a teen worker's permit, a tattered New York marriage license, an employee identification card. Here, in one envelope, along with a handful of photos found in another dresser drawer, are all the artifacts remaining of my paternal grandmother Nettie, who died in 1980 at the young age of 72. This collection of papers was what my father saved when it was his turn to do what I was now doing.

Sifting through the meager contents of this envelope, a thought arose so forcefully it was like I heard a voice saying it: *Remember, this is how it always ends.*

On Rosh Hashanah we are instructed to face our mortality. To face the fragility of life. To face the reality that our lives could be dramatically altered – or even snuffed out – in the blink of an eye. To face the reality that our lives will end, dramatically or not.

Certainly this past year we have had more than enough reminders of this reality in the news. Hurricane Sandy. Newtown, Connecticut. The Boston Marathon bombing. That's more than enough right there, although the list is much longer. I am aware of the audaciousness, the chutzpah, of my saying anything about the fragility of life in the shadow of these and other senseless tragedies. What do I know of the fragility of life, really? Yes, my parents have died, but it is within the natural order of things for parents to die. Sad, when they die "too young," but not senseless.

Statistically most of us will indeed die from natural causes, not from a random, dramatic event such as a terrorist attack. Those random events are the ones that seize our fearful attention; but for most of us, our day to day lives are not really changed by them. Our wake-up calls are more mundane: the spreading waistline, the colonoscopy, the stress test, the hip pain, the mammogram, the hearing loss. Between ourselves and our family members and friends and colleagues, we have daily reminders of the temporary nature of the body. Some may choose to believe our souls are immortal, but we have ample evidence that our bodies are absolutely mortal. Some may choose to believe in an afterlife, but Judaism is clear in emphasizing the primacy of life here and now.

Rosh Hashanah is our annual reminder of the

preciousness and fragility of life. Every year we face into the abyss, and we shudder, and perhaps we see clearly, for a moment. And then most of us go back to the sleep-walking illusion that we are somehow immune to mortality.

Sifting through the artifacts remaining of my paternal grandmother Nettie, I heard that voice saying: *Remember, this is how it always ends.* At first I found that crushing. This is how it ends? This is all there is? An envelope or maybe a box or a photo album, a few good stories retold for a generation or two if we're lucky?

Yes, this is how it always ends, and therefore there is even more urgency for *showing up* for our lives, whole -heartedly. I think of it lately as the practice of saying "yes" to life. Just a couple of weeks before my mother died, in fact, I had made a vow to take on the mindfulness practice of consciously saying "yes" at every possible opportunity. Yes to everything that happens. Yes to the simchas and the tsurris, to the joys and the sorrows. Yes even to the senseless, petty suffering that seemed to consume so much of my mother's life. How to say "yes" to all of it? How to find satisfaction and meaning in our "one wild and precious life," as the poet Mary Oliver calls it? This is the challenge of a lifetime. That is why it is called a *practice.*

The practice of saying "yes" to life whole-heartedly is the practice of accepting what *is*. The practice of saying "yes" to life whole-heartedly is the practice of daily forgiveness and compassion and letting go of our insistence that everything be how we think it ought to be, rather than how it is. It is a practice of forgiveness, and a practice of liberation.

So does that mean that we just quietly accept and say "yes" to injustice, violence, hatred, and oppression in the world without trying to change anything? Of course not. Judaism is all about paradox. On the one hand we value humility, surrender, gratitude, and acceptance of what *is*... and on the other hand we value big dreams, courageous action, and messianic transformation. Judaism is all about living in the paradox.

Now, show and tell: My father's army buttons, also found in his dresser.

My father, Jerry Robinson, served in the United States army as a young man in Lawrence Massachusetts during the Korean War. He was assigned to do scientific research, something to do with army boots and the stressful conditions they had to be constructed to withstand. But the story begins earlier.

My father was originally stationed in one of the first racially integrated units in the army. I don't recall the exact location but I know it was in the south. I don't recall him ever talking about what racial integration was like, but I do recall that on occasion it would arise in family conversation that Dad had endured anti-semitic bullying there. Mom would mention it and Dad would shrug it off. What's done is done, he would say. Water under the bridge, he would say. It was not until quite recently that I heard the story of how that anti-semitic bullying had escalated.

Here is the story as I remember it being told to me:

The announcement is made that the entire unit will be shipping out the next morning for combat duty in Korea. A list of names is posted, and all the men are listed... except Jerry Robinson. Why? Because Jerry Robinson had earned the highest score on a science aptitude test, and the commanding officers decided that his brains were needed for an Army research unit rather than combat.

Word spreads through the barracks that Jerry Robinson is being exempted from combat duty. Enraged, some of the men vow that before morning they will kill that *damn Jew*. The Christian army chaplain, hearing of this threat, hides Jerry Robinson, the Jew, overnight until all the other men are transported out the next morning.

Now if anyone has been listening to my comments about God all these years, you will understand that I do not see the hand of God in this story. This is not the story of divine intervention in the life of one man (although it is tempting to say so, especially since the hero of the story is a minister). Instead, I hear this now as a deeply tragic story on many levels. So much fear. So much hatred. And then an entire army unit of young men – boys, really – is sent off to war, all except for one randomly lucky fellow. How horrifically unfair. And also, there is something tragically absurd in the image of a chaplain saving one man from violence while hundreds more are being sent into the hell of war.

Absurd. And yet of course from the perspective of my family, this was a miraculous event.

So there is a second possible respond to the voice I heard saying, "Remember, this is how it always ends." Yes, the possessions and details and stories of our lives will be gone within a few generations; yet each of our actions ripples out into the world in all directions, affecting others now and in the future in endless and unfathomable ways.

One army chaplain, acting to protect one frightened young man, can have an impact far beyond the confines of his own little world. If it were not for the intervention of that one chaplain, my father might never have married my mother, and I would not be here today. But of course the chaplain's impact went far beyond my own egocentricity.

When my father died nine years ago, his rabbi made a point at the funeral that I have never forgotten. He said, Jerry Robinson was a quiet, straight-laced guy who lived in a very small social circle. But through his work as an adhesives chemist and inventor at Johnson & Johnson, designing bandages, my father affected – and continues to affect – hundreds of thousands of lives in hospitals around the world.

My father was never famous, just as most of us will never be famous in an Albert Einstein or Eleanor Roosevelt sort of way. Yet who he was and what he did had an impact far beyond his own little world. And his impact was built upon the impact of countless others, including my grandmother Nettie, including the United States army chaplain. This is true for all of us. This is immortality enough.

On Rosh Hashanah we are instructed to face our mortality. To face the fragility of life. To say "yes" to life whole-heartedly, while we can. And to know that who we are and what we do will have an impact far beyond our own little worlds, long after we are physically gone.

כן יהי רצון / *So may it be.*

Precious and Loveable

Kol Nidrei 2013

We stand within the community on Yom Kippur and confess the many ways we have fallen short of our own moral expectations. We even have an old custom of hitting ourselves over and over during the "ahl cheits," the communal recitation of our sins. How many of you learned that tradition growing up?

Tonight I want to talk about how to *stop* hitting ourselves.

The ten days between Rosh Hashanah and Yom Kippur are traditionally referred to as *Aseret Y'mai Teshuvah*, the ten days of teshuvah – the ten days of repentance. In the classic formulation of the laws of teshuvah, the medieval rabbi Maimonides outlined three steps: 1) the recognition of wrongdoing, 2) the experience of shame and regret, and 3) the resolve to change.

Sometimes it can seem like there is an overemphasis in Jewish tradition on the punitive aspects of teshuvah. Where in Maimonides' three-step equation, for example, is the *rachmones* – the compassion – for our less-than-perfect selves? Where is the self forgiveness? We are so endlessly hard on ourselves.

Of course sometimes we seem to be the opposite: prideful, unrepentant, sure of our rightness. But so often in those situations our bravado is just a cover up, a diversion from a deeper sense of shame. I suspect that much of the snark and negativity in our culture is also a cover-up for shame and insecurity. Where is the self forgiveness?

Over the summer, I put out a request for input on my sermon theme of Memory and Forgiveness. One temple member responded with his reflections on the necessity for self forgiveness when we are looking back on our actions and decisions. He writes:

> Who among us has never pondered what might have been had we only chosen path B instead of A? With 20/20 hindsight, the better decision seems so obvious. Why didn't we go that other route? In our quiet, reflective moments we hopefully realize that we were simply doing our best given our limitations of time, energy, aptitude and attention. We may even realize that, while the actual outcomes of decisions made are known and real to us, the might-have-beens were in the realm of fantasy, which is rose-colored by nature. In other words, we forgive ourselves and move on. Of course, these things can be easier said than done.

He writes of the situations in which we make choices and then cause ourselves suffering with endless "what ifs." Of course, there is a continuum from the simplest mistakes at one end of the spectrum to brutal crimes on the other end. The question of forgiveness is thornier when the wrongdoings are violent or malicious, when there are real victims and the consequences for those victims are irreparable. Some would argue that a person who commits a heinous crime, for example, does not deserve the peaceful heart of self forgiveness;

or certainly does not deserve it without first doing serious and credible teshuvah, including what is now referred to as restorative justice.

The possibility of forgiveness and self forgiveness in such extreme cases is a worthy topic for moral and philosophical debate. Tonight, though, let us focus on the more "mundane" mistakes and sins we commit in our everyday lives within our own families. In our everyday lives within our own families, we have ample opportunities to practice both forgiveness and self forgiveness. Another temple member rightly pointed out to me recently that forgiveness happens within the context of relationships. Practically on a daily basis, we interact with family members or caregivers in less-than-perfect ways. Practically on a daily basis, we hit ourselves for mistakes we've made in those interactions (unless we are too busy lashing out at others to avoid facing the truth of our own mistakes).

Many years ago I turned to an older friend for advice after I had made a mistake which led to another person becoming angry. My friend wrote:

> Among the people who need forgiveness, we must never forget ourselves. It is perhaps the most freeing act we can undertake, to forgive ourselves. Self forgiveness helps us grow. Remember, forgiveness does not excuse, deny or twist the truth. Forgiveness admits what is, and that stays. The fault is still there. It is not erased. In the face of that, we forgive ourselves. Then release.

I have returned to this note many times in my life since then.

Now, two things for show and tell tonight. The first thing is right here – the shofar. There is a teaching that the shape of the shofar is a metaphor for teshuvah.* One end, where the breath enters, is narrow. The other end, from which the sound emerges, is wider. We know that when we judge ourselves, there is constriction, there is a narrowing of focus which can squeeze out any possibility of kindness. We are in a tight place. Through the process of teshuvah, we can access the wider space of compassion and love. How does this happen? First we have to admit our wrong doing and leave it behind. That is the narrow end. And then we are instructed in this teaching to see ourselves as infants – as newborns – and begin again to do good deeds. In this way the punitive quality of judgment expands and widens until it is transformed into open-heartedness.

Here is the other thing for show and tell, which is directly related to this teaching about seeing ourselves as infants:

Among the possessions I inherited when my mother died this June, was a large box labeled "Grandma's photographs." This photograph of me, in this frame, was on display in my maternal grandparents' apartment in the Bronx, alongside pictures of my older brother and our cousins.

My intention in sharing this photo is not to show you how cute I was (although I was!). My intention is to remind us that every one of us begins life as a precious, lovable being. Every one of us. Yet somewhere along the way we lose touch with that truth.

And here's the secret: We still are precious and lovable. Every one of us. And so are all the people we know and work with, and so are all the people we encounter in the grocery store and in school and on the highway, and so are all the people we hear about in the news. Every one of us. B'tselem Elohim, made in the image of God. Precious and lovable.

How might we go about becoming more self forgiving? We could begin by keeping photos like this one in a prominent place in our homes. If you have children or grandchildren or other little ones in your life, of course you display their photos. So make a place in your home also for a picture like this of little you, from a time when it was completely obvious that you were a precious, lovable being.

Besides this particular photo, which brings with it such warm memories of my grandparents' apartment in the Bronx, I found a few other photos of me when I was four or five years old that are also now on display in our home. Look for the childhood pictures of yourself with bright, shining eyes that sparkle with hope and promise. That's you. That's your soul. That's your *neshama*. That's the divine spark you have been entrusted with in this lifetime. *Elohai neshama she'natata bee, tehora hee.* My God, the soul you have breathed into me, it is *pure*.

We stand within the community on Yom Kippur and confess the many ways we have fallen short of our own moral expectations. We even have an old custom of hitting ourselves over and over during the recitation of our sins. This year, let our self assessment be laser sharp in its honesty. Let us not shrink from the bright light of inquiry into our wrongdoings. And then when our assessment feels complete, let us picture our precious, lovable selves in our mind's eye, and open our fists into a caress. Because the truth is that at any given moment in our lives, we – precious, lovable beings – are doing the best we can.

And may it be that the next time we do something unskillful for which we need to do teshuvah, we can sit with that image of our precious, lovable selves, and forgive ourselves, and move on.

כן יהי רצון / *So may it be.*

---

* From *Torey Zahav* (Binyamin ben Aharon of Zalocze, d. 1791), quoted in *Speaking Torah*, Arthur Green, Jewish Lights 2013

The Big Picture

Yom Kippur 2013

When I was in fifth grade, my friend K beat me up.

I say she beat me up, because that was the expression in those days. It was actually a series of incidents over perhaps a week or two. An angry shove when the teacher's back was turned, another shove down the stairs on the way to gym; and then finally, in the hallway after school, hair-pulling and punches in the stomach. I stood there, baffled and afraid, taking the blows. "Stop it," I said. "Stop it," she mimicked. Another friend came over and hugged me, making herself into a shield. K just punched her in the back instead. Eventually, K must have walked away; I don't remember how it ended. I do remember that no adult saw or intervened, and no child in the crowded hallway thought to seek an adult's assistance. We were in our own world. Fifth grade.

During this high holiday season, we are instructed to seek out people who we have wronged and ask for their forgiveness. Our ancient rabbis even recorded in the Talmud detailed instructions such as the obligation to ask for forgiveness up to three times before giving up. It seems to me, though, that the instructions are less clear for what exactly the forgiver is supposed to do, beyond saying "I forgive you."

I don't know about you, but my life experience thus far has been that bestowing forgiveness is not so simple. "I forgive you." Does that do it? Are words sufficient? Is it ever possible to know if forgiveness is sincere, and complete?

Forgiveness is one of the mysteries of the human heart.

There is a prayer traditionally recited every night before bedtime which begins with these words:

> Ribono shel Olam, Master of the Universe, I hereby forgive anyone who angered or antagonized me or who sinned against me – whether against my body, my property, my honor or against anything of mine; whether they did so accidentally, willfully, carelessly, or purposely; whether through speech, deed, thought, or fantasy; whether in this transmigration or another transmigration – I forgive every person....

In my experience, the daily practice of reciting this bedtime prayer can be humbling. Try it some time for a few months, or even just a few days. You earnestly forgive someone Monday night, say, and then find on Tuesday night that actually you have to admit there is still some sense of disappointment or betrayal arising in your mind, and so you forgive them again. And then perhaps they turn up again in your thoughts as you recite this prayer a few days or weeks later, just when you think maybe today your list of grievances is finally cleared. There is great wisdom in making this a daily prayer. If we are honest with ourselves, bestowing forgiveness turns out not to be a one-time thing.

What is the opposite or the absence of forgiveness? The certainty and aloneness of being right.

I have been thinking a lot about forgiveness since my mother died this June. Even in the best of mother/daughter relationships, there is much to forgive; and ours was not the best of mother/daughter relationships. What some of you witnessed these last two years was my mother at her best psychologically (although obviously at her worst physically). What some of you witnessed these last two years was the culmination of a decades-long, and yet still painfully incomplete, process of forgiveness. And as I foresaw, the process of both seeking and bestowing forgiveness continues after her death.

What is the nature of forgiveness? Do we make it happen, or is it an experience of grace?

Sorting through mom's possessions this summer, I came upon a pile of notes I had written to her throughout my childhood. One note was folded up small with the words "Mom only! Urgent! Private!" written on the outside. This note offers another glimpse into my fifth grade experience of being beaten up by my friend:

> Dear Mom,
>
> I have a bad problem in school. You know that mean girl K I told you about. Well in school today she was pulling my hair and hitting me, and when I asked why she didn't answer. Mary told me that K is mad because when I'm late, the teacher doesn't

say anything to me; but when K's late the teacher yells at her. All the kids say I should fight back or tell you so you could call her mother, but I don't think it would help if you called her mother because then she would be sore at me for telling on her. Donna says her mother called up K's mother when K was bothering her and she left her alone, but I don't think it will help me any. Please do something, or tell me what to do, I just can't stand it! She punches! Please!

Everyone is familiar with the kaddish prayer, right? *Yitgadal v'yitkadash sh'may raba.* "Magnified and sanctified be God's great name." Kaddish is traditionally recited by mourners at the conclusion of every service, although the prayer itself says nothing about death.

Yitgadal v'yitkadash. Kaddish is called kaddish because of that second word, yitkadash. Kuf-dalet-shin, the Hebrew and Aramaic root that means holy, sanctified. But the first word interests me more. Yitgadal. From the root gimel-dalet-lamed. To enlarge. To make bigger. Or as the standard translation puts it, to "magnify." The first word of the kaddish challenges us to *make God bigger*.

What do you mean, make God bigger? Isn't God already the essence of bigness? As I recite kaddish every day this year in memory of my mother, I am realizing that kaddish is a daily reminder: Every time we think we know what God is, that's not it. God is bigger. Every time we are in awe of someone or something, and feel drawn into submission or worship, that's not God. God is bigger. In every situation where we feel wronged or hurt and think we know what happened, that's not it. The situation is bigger. Every time we recite – *yit-barach v'yish-tabach v'yit-pa'ar v'yit-romam v'yit-naseh v'yit-hadar v'yit-aleh v'yit-halal* – every one of those words is about going deeper, higher, grander, bigger, wider! We are being challenged by the kaddish to expand our perspective, to expand our consciousness.

What is the nature of forgiveness? For me, an essential part of forgiveness is this process of enlarging our perspective. Astronauts speak of the "overview effect," a shift in consciousness they experience when viewing the entire planet Earth from space. We don't have to be astronauts. We can fly upward in our imagination. Imagine flying upward, the view below expanding out in all directions.

The process of forgiveness involves an interior shift of perspective, flying upward in our imagination to see the bigger picture of a situation. With a bigger picture, the larger context of peoples' actions and motives comes into view. The more context we can see, the more empathy we can experience. The more empathy, the more compassion. And compassion – tapping our common humanity – is at the heart of forgiveness.

This is not to say that wrong-doing is excusable or justifiable. A punch in the stomach is still a punch in the stomach. There is a good reason why the entire high holidays prayer book is filled with images of God as both judging *and* compassionate. Our tradition understands the necessity for balance, the necessity for living within the paradox.

Flying high above the Earth leads to an enlarged, breathtaking view of the whole planet. Flying much, much further away leads to seeing the planet as what Carl Sagan refers to as a "pale blue dot." From this far distant vantage point we achieve not only the big picture but also a profound sense of our own smallness.

The spiritual work of being human involves cultivating both perspectives. Just as we are challenged to enlarge and magnify God, so too we are challenged to make ourselves smaller. To humble ourselves. To become Nothing relative to God. Our sages call it "nullifying the Ego." Especially during the high holidays, we aim to nullify our ego before the One who our ancestors called "king of kings." This, our mystics tell us, is the essence of our task as humans: to lessen our ego relative to God. To comprehend and acknowledge our place within all of existence.

Astronauts speak of the overview effect. Carl Sagan speaks of the pale blue dot. Judaism speaks of God as "ayn sof," without end, the mystics' name for the divine totality of existence. Ayn sof, within which we are but tiny, momentary manifestations of divine energy. From this perspective – from God's perspective – who is forgiving who, really? Who or what is the "I," the me that imagines that it is bestowing forgiveness on someone else?

Hearing the story of K beating me up in fifth grade, it would be understandable to frame the situation in terms of my need to forgive K for what she did to me. Well, yes and no. Let us now fly up a bit above this story, and you will see that it is far from clear who was in need of forgiving whom:

Fifth grade. The school year is 1968-1969. Our fifth grade teacher, Mrs. A, is a pretty young newlywed in her twenties who does needlepoint and plays guitar and teaches us to sing "Kumbaya" and "We Shall Overcome" without explaining why. Mrs. A is white. My friend K is black, and lives in a different part of our little town than all my other friends who are white. Differentiating skin color is not, however, a part of my consciousness as a ten-year-old. K and I have been school friends since I moved to town two years earlier, and all I know is that suddenly she is angry.

Unbeknownst to me, my mother does not call K's mother the next morning; my mother calls Mr. Snow the principal. Mr. Snow speaks with Mrs. A the teacher. Mrs. A calls both of us up to her desk to gently – with a smile and a joke – reprimand us both for fighting.

Now who was in need of forgiveness in this story? Was it K, or Mrs. A, or my mother, or the principal, or me… or the wider society in which white privilege was the norm?

Even in a liberal town with sympathetic, well-meaning teachers like Mrs. A, the inequities that K was responding to with anger in 1968 played out in many ways in our school system over the years that followed. Already by the following year, in middle school, we were "tracked" into different classes. By high school, I only saw her and the other black girls in gym class and the cafeteria, and by then we were self-segregating.

As my academic opportunities widened, K's probably narrowed. She may never have gone to college. If she did, it was probably not to a costly Ivy League university. She's not on Facebook; a Google search yields only her address and phone number. Flying high above this situation in both space and time, we can see the bigger picture of two vastly different life trajectories within a society that is still struggling to right the injustice of racial prejudice.

Forgiveness, then, is ultimately about flying high enough above a situation that our view encompasses the biggest possible picture. Forgiveness is also about flying even higher, gaining a perspective far beyond our own little ego.

This is the spiritual work of being human. On the micro and the macro scale. In daily life and in global affairs. In families and in nations; and in our own hearts.

Yitgadal v'yitkadash sh'may raba. Amen.

What Can One Person Do? Part 1

Erev Rosh Hashanah 2014

This summer, I added my maiden name to my Facebook name. I wanted to post something on a "chitchat" page for people from my home town in New Jersey, and I knew that no one would recognize me by the name Kafka.

A week or so later, I received a Facebook message from a man living in New York State. He wrote:

> Dear Randy, over these many years since high school, you have popped into my mind more than a few times. I can't tell you now why this is so except to say that something must have triggered a memory. I write you now because, for the first time, a Facebook post of yours popped up on my news feed. What a treat to see you and know you are well. I remember well that, as a freshman, slogging along and trying to figure out high school and my place in it, you were uncommonly nice and helpful to me, and I never forgot that. I do not know if you remember this, but despite not being in the same grade we did develop a nice school friendship. You graduated and I stayed behind to finish out the rest of high school. Lost track of you and that's only natural. Thanks for being a friend way back when."

And then of course he went on to fill me in about his work and family and where they live, etc.

I share this story with you tonight not to pat myself on

the back, but because it is one answer to the question I am raising this year: "What can one person do?" As you will hear in my upcoming sermons, I am generally framing the question in terms of what one person can do in the face of the many troubling urgencies that compete for our attention and energy.

But tonight I want to focus the question a bit differently. In some ways, tonight I am just picking up where I left off last Rosh Hashanah morning. Last Rosh Hashanah I made the observation that each of our actions ripples out into the world in all directions, affecting others now and in the future in endless and unfathomable ways. I shared the story of the army chaplain who saved my father from the violent, antisemitic rage of his peers. And I shared the story of the rabbi's eulogy at my father's funeral 10 years ago, in which the rabbi noted that my father's anonymous work as an adhesives chemist at Johnson & Johnson ultimately affected hundreds of thousands of lives in hospitals around the world. We *all* have the potential to influence the lives of others in countless ways.

This summer I had two such reminders of my own, albeit on a smaller scale. First, this Facebook message, coming to me after an encounter that happened *40 years ago*. That I was kind to a freshman boy 40 years ago made a difference in his life in ways that neither of us could have imagined at the time.

My second story happened a bit earlier this summer. All this past year, I had been dimly aware that the synagogue in Randolph had an interim rabbi, but our paths somehow never crossed.

In June, just as his interim contract was ending, I happened to come upon his name in a newspaper article online. I recognized the name immediately – It was my beloved Hebrew School teacher from when I was 11 years old! He had been around 22 years old at the time, a rabbinical student at Jewish Theological Seminary who had grown up in my home town. My parents were acquainted with his parents; and in the decades since then my mother had occasionally mentioned him when news of his rabbinic career appeared in the local paper.

When I contacted him this summer, he said he absolutely remembered me! We got together twice for lunch, and talked for hours each time. Each of us had an impact on the other that we did not realize until 44 years later. He remembered me as being sweet and respectful (his words) in an otherwise rambunctious Hebrew School class that did him in after only one year. And in my 11-year-old eyes, he modeled that it was possible to be a cool young adult who was also passionate about living a Jewish life.

But beyond that brief encounter 44 years ago, we both acknowledged the incredible emotional debt we have to our rabbi, Yakov Hilsenrath, may his memory be a blessing, who died this past February. That each of us became rabbis, each in our own way, was a direct outgrowth of our relationship to this man. But Rabbi Hilsenrath's influence went far beyond our career choices.

What can one person do? My rabbi was a force of nature. You probably have not heard of him – he wasn't "famous" beyond the world of Conservative

Judaism – but I know that he impacted the lives of countless people. He was a man of fierce integrity, deeply rooted in his traditional Orthodox Jewish upbringing in Europe. He always understood ethical principles to be mitzvot in the traditional sense of *commandments*. Was he perfect? Of course not. But he was a mensch, and has been an inspirational role model for me in many ways.

Two stories about what a mensch my rabbi was:

First – When I was a young teen, my father lost his job at Johnson and Johnson and a few months later had a heart attack. He was in his 40s. When Rabbi Hilsenrath heard about my father's situation, he contacted a temple *macher* [important person] who also happened to be a macher at J&J. The rabbi urged this macher to help my father find a new position in a different division – and he did. My father remained with the company until his retirement. My mother always considered the rabbi's intervention to be an act of *pikuach nefesh* – the saving of a life. I knew nothing of this at the time, and only heard about it years later.

My mother also told me years later that Rabbi Hilsenrath offered to pay for me to go on a trip to Israel while my father was recovering that summer. She ruefully recalled decades later that she had been afraid that I would visit Israel and become "too Jewish," so she never even told me about the offer!

The other Rabbi Hilsenrath mensch story is even more personal. When Alan and I first met and fell in love 32 years ago, my parents objected. Hurtful words were spoken, tears were shed, anger and frustration built up on both sides of a growing chasm. There seemed no way out of the crisis.

Alan and I requested a meeting with Rabbi Hilsenrath to express our frustration and helplessness. He said he would handle my parents. To this day we do not know what he said to them. But whatever he said to them had the desired effect, and Rabbi Hilsenrath officiated at our wedding a year later.

You all have stories like mine. What can one person do? You know: Act kindly towards someone who is new, or struggling. Be a role model for a young person. Live a life of integrity. Strive to be a mensch. You just might change the course of someone's life.

And one more thing…

We often focus over the high holidays on the obligation to apologize for any wrongs we may have committed whether intentionally or not. This year, let us add the obligation to express gratitude to someone who has made a positive difference in our lives.

Express gratitude. Even if many years have passed, reach out and thank someone for the positive impact they made in your life. Don't wait until you are writing it as a condolence note to the person's surviving family members.

May we all strive in the coming year to be a mensch, and to express gratitude to the menschs who have enriched our lives.

כן יהי רצון / *So may it be.*

What Can One Person Do? Part 2

Rosh Hashanah 2014

Five years ago, at our first Rosh Hashanah as a newly-merged Temple Kol Tikvah, I shared my suggestions for three core values worth cultivating. They might have been entirely forgotten if Randy O'Brien had not thought to immortalize them as a beautiful challah cover:

"Love more. Learn more. Fix what's broken."

In honor of this being Kol Tikvah's fifth year, I went back to take a look at that very first sermon. Not surprisingly, I have a different perspective than I did five years ago. (And I hope that I will have yet another perspective five years from now!) This year, I am drawn to focus on the "fix what's broken," and in a different way than I did five years ago.

As many of you know, this past February I went on a 10-day tour of Rwanda to witness some of the peace-building efforts that have been evolving there since the Tutsi genocide 20 years ago. It was a mind-blowing journey. I shared some of my reflections on my blog, and also gave a presentation in May. (For anyone who missed it, the video of my talk is on the temple website.) Ever since the trip, I have been wrestling with the question: What can one person do?

What can one person do? Within the worldview of

Jewish tradition, human beings always have a moral choice. We read in the Torah: "Behold I set before you this day blessing and curse, life and death – therefore choose life." Over and over, both in the Torah and in rabbinic tradition throughout our history, freedom of moral choice is a given. In our worldview, perpetrators of evil are free moral agents, not helpless pawns. And, conversely, individuals can and do choose to do good in the face of evil.

In Rwanda, my travel companions and I heard plenty of stories of death, but we also heard many stories of people who have chosen *life*. People who have chosen to live side-by-side with former enemies, in some cases to reconcile, in some cases even to forgive – even to love – in the face of evil. This is the choice that to some of us seems incomprehensible. Just as we cannot wrap our minds around how ordinary people could become barbarous murderers, so too we cannot wrap our minds around how ordinary people can heal from unbearable suffering enough to actually forgive their tormentors. Both seem equally mysterious. Yet it appears that both genocide and tolerance evolve in predictable ways, and can therefore be either encouraged or stifled. And this is ultimately a hopeful message, both for the people of Rwanda and for all of us.

"Behold I set before you this day blessing and curse, life and death." Humanity seems to hold such potential for divine exaltation and glory, and yet seems still to be so profoundly *animal* in its potential for cruelty and murderous violence.

We may wish for it to be otherwise – and we are

obligated to strive to make it otherwise – and simultaneously we must acknowledge that our vision of peace and justice is as yet but a vision. Judaism teaches us to hope for and work towards that messianic vision; yet we cannot deny that humanity today is not only theoretically capable of mass destruction, it has manifested such mass destruction countless times. Lethal weapons in the hands of humans only recently evolved a step beyond animals constitute a deadly threat to all that is beautiful and good in the world. We would be naïve to think otherwise.

We humans are so small, so precious, so capable of divine goodness and at the same time of unspeakable cruelty. The choice is always ours.

So what can one person do?

When it feels as if the Dark Side is rising around the world, when it feels as if hatred and violence and cruel injustices are oozing up through every crack of human nature... the question arises: What can one person do?

The question arises out of the eternal paradox of hope and despair – the paradox we Jews carry with us throughout our lives and throughout history.

Sometimes the question comes out as an expression of despair, spoken with a sigh: What can one person do? Implicit in asking it that way is the belief that one person cannot do anything of significance in the face of evil.

But the question can also come from a place of hope, as a call to action. What can one person do?

There are in this world an overwhelming number of

urgencies being flung into our faces daily. There is an almost addictive quality to the sense of shock and outrage that we are urged to feel multiple times a day via internet and television news and viral postings on social media. Click. Gasp. Click. Gasp. Click.... And on it goes, day after day.

What can one person do?

It seems to me that we have a variety of options. The first is to become numb. To turn away from the urgent needs of others both locally and around the world. To tune it all out, because it's just too much and too overwhelming. This is a very real option; and I admit that at times I have been there. I imagine that we all have. And that's okay, as long as we don't stay there.

Another option is to become an activist for social change. Some people seem to have the gift for activism, for rallying crowds and organizing communities, for public speaking and lobbying and advocating and creating large-scale cultural shifts.

And then there are all the options along the continuum between those two poles, the options for most of us. We can for example be clicktivists, signing petitions or sharing internet posts as part of a larger movement. Or we can be the front-line workers and volunteers, doing the hands-on work that needs doing. Or we can be fund-raisers and philanthropists, a time-honored way to respond to urgencies by supporting the workers and volunteers and activists.

We can also become worriers. We can wring our hands about all the urgent troubles in the world, and feel that somehow our anxiety is proof that we care and that we are engaged; although in reality we aren't actually doing anything, and in fact our worrying only serves to wear down our bodies and spirits.

If you are an activist, or a clicktivist, or a philanthropist, or a volunteer, please know that what you are doing makes a difference. Personally, I sometimes feel intimidated and envious of my activist colleagues who manifest their Jewish values on a larger public stage than I do. But then I remind myself (or my husband reminds me) that the world needs contemplative introverts too! The world needs people who make a difference one human interaction at a time, not just broad social movements and revolutions.

When we become numb, or when all we do is generate unproductive anxiety, we can take one small step back into the world of action: We can pick *one thing to actively care about*. One thing. It could be a small, local urgency or a bigger one. I cannot tell you what to care about. Only your heart can tell you that, and perhaps it already has. Or perhaps not, yet.

There is a Jewish mystical teaching that each of us is here to discover and then to do the particular *tikkun* we were born to do. Tikkun means repair or fixing. This teaching answers the age-old question "Why are we here?" by suggesting that we are here to fix something only we can fix. And how do we learn what that is? Counter-intuitively, this teaching suggests that we learn what we are uniquely meant to fix by looking with curiosity at the aspect of life in which we are struggling the most. What is difficult for us? What is problematic, vexing, troubling? That is the hint that we are getting closer to clarifying the tikkun we alone are called to do. This process of clarification may be a life-long process. It is simultaneously a call to action. And we don't have to buy into the mystical aspect of this teaching completely in order to benefit from its message.

One final note: A reminder that Judaism takes the long view. Our ancient sages taught us: "It is not for you to complete the work, but neither are you free to walk away from it." Another way to express the long view comes from a story in the Talmud: A traveler is journeying on the road and comes upon a person planting a carob tree. The traveler asks how long it takes for such trees to bear fruit. The person replies, "Seventy years." Perplexed, the traveler asks, "Are you certain that you will live another seventy years?" The person replies: "I found ready-grown carob trees in the world; as my ancestors planted for me, so I now plant for my children." [Ta'anit 23a]

So when it feels as if the Dark Side is rising around the world, when it feels as if hatred and violence and cruel injustices are oozing up through every crack of human nature... what can one person do? Listen to your heart for an answer, and then go do it.

What Can One Person Do? Part 3

Kol Nidrei 2014

About 23 years ago, Alan and I and our then toddler Jacob attended the 60th birthday party of a good friend. After a few hours, as people began saying their goodbyes and leaving the party, we overheard our friend say "Oh, people are leaving. I guess that's what's happening now." Just like that. No judgment, no sadness, no wishing for it to be otherwise. Just "Oh, I guess that's what's happening now." Ever since then, that expression has been a guiding spiritual principle in our family (as well as, on occasion, a source of humor). Our good friend is now in his 80s, and he too continues to try to live by that principle, day by day. Whatever is happening now, that's what's happening. Wishing it were otherwise only causes suffering.

Of course, being human, we also experience the flip side of that guiding spiritual principle: Whatever is happening now… it could be better!

In the Jewish tradition we have a name for these paradoxical impulses: netsach and hod.

Netsach can be understood as the drive to change the world – striding forward and making a difference. Netsach is courageous action, self-confidence, dreaming big, believing in the possibility of transformation.

Hod, in contrast, can be understood as the quality of acceptance. Hod manifests as gratitude, surrender, humility. But hod is not resignation or depression, or giving up or giving in, or being a doormat. Hod is often expressed through silence.

There is a traditional map of psycho-spiritual qualities known in Jewish mysticism as the tree of life – which is understood to be both a metaphorical categorizing of God's qualities as well as a map of the human psyche. On the tree of life, netsach and hod are dynamic polarities.

This holiday season I am asking the question, What can one person do? On Rosh Hashanah, and again tomorrow morning, my focus is primarily on responding to the many urgencies in the world with *action*. Yet our tradition teaches us to value the *balancing* of netsach and hod. So tonight I would like to lift up the benefits of hod.

Here is one perspective on life that comes from the side of hod. It is the perspective on life that comes to me when I sit by the ocean:

Each of us, all of us, all of humanity, are but tiny droplets in the huge ocean of Life. Tiny, tiny droplets. All of our personal dramas, our joys and sorrows – all droplets in the huge ocean of Life.

In the Yizkor service we recite these ancient words: Adonai, mah Adam va-tayda-ayhoo... "God, what is a human that you are mindful of it? A human is like an empty breath – its days are like a passing shadow. In the morning it shoots up like grass, and in the evening fades and withers."

The modern Reform translation we use has shifted the

language of this passage to a more comfortable 2nd person plural – "God, what are we that you are mindful of us?" But in fact the original Hebrew is more striking in its insistence that the grand sweep of life and death is impersonal. It just is.

And the tumultuous world events that capture our anxious attention these days? Syria? Iraq? Nigeria? Ukraine? Israel? All waves. Waves, never-ending waves in the grand oceanic sweep of human history.

And human history itself is but a tiny wave amidst the vast ocean of time and energy that is the unfathomable universe which some of us call God. This is what the medieval language of our high holiday prayers seems to be trying to point us towards – the awesome, unknowable grandeur of ultimate Reality.

We might be tempted to conclude from this perspective that our individual attempts to make a difference are laughable. In the "grand scheme of things," what difference does it make what we choose to do or not do? But I believe that a more compelling conclusion to reach from viewing our lives from this cosmic perspective is the necessity for cultivating compassion. Compassion for ourselves and for one another. Compassion for this crazy predicament we call being human.

Bringing this down to the personal level: Implicit and explicit in the customs surrounding the high holidays is the message that we are supposed to "get our act together," that we are supposed to DO something to shift the direction we are headed in, that we are supposed to do teshuvah – examining our past actions and intending to behave differently in the future. We are supposed to explore our regrets about our own behaviors, as well as our resentments about other people's behaviors, and resolve to make amends, forgive, or in some way make a *change*. But what if change is not the whole story? Sometimes I think our tradition around the high holidays is too much netsach and not enough hod. Sometimes I think that we are too focused on the assumption that we have to change, that we have to fix ourselves somehow. But what if we are okay as is? What if part of teshuvah has to do with facing and *accepting* our imperfect selves?

This is the hidden gift of Yom Kippur – expressed in traditional language as the inevitability of being forgiven by God by tomorrow evening. This is why some of us have the custom of experiencing Yom Kippur as a joyful holiday rather than a grim one. Yes, it can be a time of introspection and self-scrutiny. Yet there is also the potential for radical forgiveness – for letting go – if only for a moment – of our incessant desire for ourselves and other people to be somehow better or different than who we are right now. We are all, right now, doing the best we can. Paradoxically, Yom Kippur offers us this gift.

Out of the creative tension that arises in balancing the qualities of netsach and hod day by day, a third quality is manifested: Yesod. This quality is also called the Tsaddik – the righteous one. It is the quality of maturity, of moral discernment, of being both strong and flexible in the face of conflict. It is the wisdom that comes in knowing when to act and when to be still.

And from Yesod flows the creative energy and love with which we build relationships and communities.

As we enter into this holy, precious day of Yom Kippur, this day of atonement, may we also catch a glimpse of the balance of Yesod. May the divine qualities of netsach and hod manifest in our lives in a fruitful balance which leads to the flowering of loving relationships and a deepening sense of community. May we all cultivate the wisdom of the tsaddik, the righteous one, in discerning when to act and when to be still. And may we all be able to say, with wisdom and with joy, "Oh, I guess that's what's happening now."

כן יהי רצון / *So may it be.*

What Can One Person Do? Part 4

Yom Kippur 2014

This has been a painful year. A sometimes frightening, sometimes overwhelming year. A difficult year to be a rational optimist, which is what I like to consider myself. This has been a year of enemies, some with names we have never heard of before, names like ISIS, Boko Haram, Khorasan. On the continuum of hope and despair, this has perhaps been a year with more despair than we have experienced in a long while. And not only for Jews. For people of color in the United States, for example, and for their allies who believe in the American vision of justice, it has been a year of outrage, fear, and at times despair.

As I said on Rosh Hashanah: When it feels as if the Dark Side is rising around the world, when it feels as if hatred and violence and cruel injustices are oozing up through every crack of human nature.... The question arises: What can one person do?

What can one person do?

Today I would like to share with you a wisdom teaching from the early rabbinic master Hillel, which provides a framework for answering this question. It also contains within it a comprehensive blueprint for living a moral life:

> If I am not for myself, who will be for me?
>
> Yet if I am for myself alone, what am I?
>
> And if not now, when?

This three-line teaching, about 2000 years old, encapsulates the entire particularism/universalism paradox we experience in Judaism. Are we obligated to take care of ourselves? Yes. That's particularism. Are we obligated to take care of others? Yes. That's universalism. And in both cases, we are obligated to *act*, not simply to believe or philosophize.

As some of you may have noticed over the years, I tend not to talk about world events or political situations either in my sermons or in conversation. By temperament and conviction, I am drawn to the interpersonal/psychological/spiritual realm – contemplating the human condition, sharing Jewish teachings about how best to live a meaningful life, how best to love and care for one another, how best to handle personal crises and suffering with grace and wisdom.

Which is not to say that I am unconcerned with world events, nor putting my proverbial head in the sand. In truth, I am often absorbed in contemplation of world events, but for me that usually leads back to the contemplation of the human condition.

On this Yom Kippur, I feel challenged to speak of both world events *and* the human condition.

You may not know this, but every summer, rabbis receive a steady flow of emails and letters from organizations urging that we give sermons on particular hot button issues. This summer, just to name a *few* examples, I was urged to focus on: climate change, gun control, torture and other human rights abuses such as human trafficking and solitary confinement, violence against women, the persistence of racism, antisemitism, and of course Israel. A grim list indeed.

From all these issues, I feel most drawn to share my thoughts about Israel.

There has been much talk over the past few years about the difficulties rabbis experience in speaking about Israel from the pulpit. About the difficulties American Jews have in speaking with each other about Israel at all, actually. Many rabbis are choosing not to mention Israel at all, for fear of offending someone in their congregation. I even heard of a congregation which has made it official policy that *no one* speaks about Israel from the bima. No one.

I am grateful every day that Kol Tikvah is a place where I can trust that you will listen to what I have to say with an open heart and an open mind.

And don't worry, I have no intention of engaging in armchair political strategizing, right, left, or otherwise. My fluctuating opinions are no more worthy of attention than anyone else's, and certainly not worthy of your attention on this holiest day in the Jewish year.

But turning back to Hillel's teaching helps me to frame what I do feel called to say about Israel.

First: If I am not for myself, who am I? Read the "myself" here as referring to the Jewish people. If we Jews are not concerned about the welfare of other Jews, than who are we? Identifying as a Jew is meaningless unless it translates into an identification with other Jews. We are a people, however dimly we may comprehend what that means.

To put it more bluntly and cynically: Whether we feel ourselves to be a part of and therefore responsible for the Jewish people or not, what happens in Israel effects all of us. Whether we endorse the particular policies of the Israeli government or not, what happens in Israel effects all of us. We would be naïve to think otherwise. Jews in Europe felt this far more acutely this summer than those of us living in the privileged, liberal bubble of Massachusetts, as they experienced first-hand the antisemitic outbursts which so often follow Israeli military actions.

During this recent time of war, Jews all over the world trembled, and no doubt many felt a heightened sense of connection to and concern for Israel. AND thoughtful, well-meaning people – both in Israel and the diaspora – differ drastically in their opinions about what led to the war, even about who "won," and certainly about what can and ought to happen next.

Israel needs our support. As a follower of Hillel's teaching, I agree with this assertion. AND thoughtful, well-meaning people differ drastically in their opinions about what constitutes "supporting" Israel. Does "supporting" mean unwavering public and financial support for every decision made by the Israeli government and its military? By that definition, the majority of *Israelis* do not always "support" Israel! The Jewish people have a proud four-thousand-year legacy of engaging in dispute. There are many, many ways to express love of and engagement with the people and the land of Israel, including respectfully protesting some of its government's policies and actions – just as we regularly protest our own government's policies and actions.

One example of a situation in Israeli society where loving support for Israel might (and already does) include respectful protest: If you go beyond the mainstream media, you will hear Israeli voices (including the official voice of the Reform movement in Israel) expressing alarm over the increasingly anti-democratic tone that has seeped into the national discourse as well as the legislative process. Never mind for the moment the experience of Palestinians – some *Jews* in Israel are experiencing a chilling movement to suppress dissent, free speech, and some basic human rights. It is important for us to know that diaspora support of these liberal Zionist values does make a difference in Israel.

So yes, by all means support Israel. And follow your conscience in determining *how* to express your support, and what aspects and movements within Israel you feel drawn to support in the name of Israel's continuing survival. Israel is a multi-vocal, complex, vibrant, and imperfect society – find your own way to connect and be supportive. Disengagement and despair are no longer valid options. I am saying this not only to you, but to myself as well. What happens in Israel effects all of us.

But turning back to Hillel's teaching, there is more to say.

I have spoken often of the particularist/universalist

paradox in Judaism. Lines one and two of Hillel's teaching capture the paradox perfectly. Take a look at the second line now, so conveniently neglected by Jewish particularists, especially during times of war and conflict:

Yet if I am for myself alone, what am I?

Rabbinic commentators throughout the centuries have noted that the shift to asking "what" am I rather than "who" am I hints that if we do not care for others, we risk losing our humanity. We risk becoming like animals, or like inanimate objects.

For some of us this summer, concern for the welfare of civilians in Gaza seemed obvious. Yet for many others, fear of the Other eclipsed even this basic level of human decency.

I want to share with you a story that for me captures the danger of extreme particularism. And I am speaking here primarily of the danger to our souls – again, I want to be clear that I make no pretense of expressing opinions regarding specific political and military strategy. My concern is for the soul of the Jewish people, and I believe there is reason for concern.

So, a story: This summer, there was a huge pro-Israel rally in New York City. Thousands of people carried identical posters saying "I stand with Israel" and "We are all Israel." Among the crowd were a few rabbis who held those signs, but who also held small signs saying "No more dead" and "Stand with Israel, Mourn with Gaza." Among those rabbis was an Israeli rabbi, son of a former Israeli consul general and nephew of a former chief rabbi of Israel. Some people at the rally – other Jews – became verbally abusive and tried to rip the rabbi's sign, telling him that he should go die in Gaza, or die in the gas chambers. When a Jewish woman called him a mamzer, a bastard, the rabbi asked her to show respect to his father who is a Holocaust survivor. The woman responded: "He should have died so you would not have been born."*

As some of you may know, my journey to Rwanda this past February included not only the ten day trip itself, but also months of study both before and after the trip. Study which brought me full-circle to my early roots in social psychology. From this immersive experience I learned that genocidal ideology evolves along a continuum, and that there are personal moral choices being made at every step along that continuum. Classification of Us versus Them is an early step on the path; later comes dehumanization, organizing into hate groups, followed by further demonizing of the Other. We Jews know of these stages only too well; many of us have developed finely-tuned antennas for catching even the earliest hint of antisemitic ideology in a person or in a society. That there are Jews today making choices which place *themselves* on this continuum of hatred and violence is an irony almost too painful to bear.

Hillel's teaching is a useful measure of our humanity. If we become so narrow and fearful that we care only about ourselves, we risk dehumanizing others. And with dehumanization comes a descent into the dark side. "If I am for myself alone, what am I?"

There is an ancient midrash, a rabbinic teaching, about the sound of the shofar. It is said to resemble the sound of mournful weeping and wailing. Who is weeping? One tradition says it is our ancestor Sarah, crying out when she hears that her husband Abraham is on his way to sacrifice their son Isaac. That's particularism, concern for our own. But a parallel rabbinic tradition says it is the mournful cry of Cicera's mother. The cry of our enemy's mother, fearful that her son has been killed in battle against us. That our sages would choose to recall the cry of our enemy's mother at the holiest time in our calendar is an expression of universalism, of compassion for all of humanity. It is a reminder that a grief-stricken mother is a grief-stricken mother, no matter what nationality she is.

What can one person do? May it be that in the coming year, we all strive to find a living balance between particularism and universalism. May we renew our commitment to caring for our fellow Jews, AND may we renew our commitment to bettering the lives of *all* people. And if not now, when?

* Story reported in *The Forward* by Hody Nemes, July 30, 2014